T0222818

Programming Web Applications with Node, Express and Pug

Jörg Krause

Apress®

Programming Web Applications with Node, Express and Pug

Jörg Krause
Berlin, Germany

ISBN-13 (pbk): 978-1-4842-2510-3   ISBN-13 (electronic): 978-1-4842-2511-0
DOI 10.1007/978-1-4842-2511-0

Library of Congress Control Number: 2016961762

Managing Director: Welmoed Spahr
Acquisitions Editor: Louise Corrigan
Editorial Board: Steve Anglin, Pramila Balan, Laura Berendson, Aaron Black, Louise Corrigan, Jonathan Gennick, Todd Green, Robert Hutchinson, Celestin Suresh John, Nikhil Karkal, James Markham, Susan McDermott, Matthew Moodie, Natalie Pao, Gwenan Spearing
Coordinating Editor: Nancy Chen
Copy Editor: Larissa Shmailo
Compositor: SPi Global
Indexer: SPi Global
Artist: SPi Global

Distributed to the book trade worldwide by Springer Science+Business Media New York, 233 Spring Street, 6th Floor, New York, NY 10013. Phone 1-800-SPRINGER, fax (201) 348-4505, e-mail orders-ny@springer-sbm.com, or visit www.springer.com. Apress Media, LLC is a California LLC and the sole member (owner) is Springer Science + Business Media Finance Inc (SSBM Finance Inc). SSBM Finance Inc is a **Delaware** corporation.

For information on translations, please e-mail rights@apress.com, or visit www.apress.com.

Apress and friends of ED books may be purchased in bulk for academic, corporate, or promotional use. eBook versions and licenses are also available for most titles. For more information, reference our Special Bulk Sales–eBook Licensing web page at www.apress.com/bulk-sales.

Any source code or other supplementary materials referenced by the author in this text are available to readers at www.apress.com. For detailed information about how to locate your book's source code, go to www.apress.com/source-code/. Readers can also access source code at SpringerLink in the Supplementary Material section for each chapter.

Printed on acid-free paper

Contents at a Glance

Contents

About the Author

Jörg Krause has been working with software and software technology since the early 1980's, beginning with a ZX 81 and taking his first steps as a programmer in BASIC and assembly language. He studied Information Technology at Humboldt University, Berlin but left early, in the 90's, to start his own company. He has worked with Internet Technology and software development since the early days when CompuServe and FidoNet dominated. He's been with Microsoft technologies and software since Windows 95.

In 1998, he worked on one of the first commercial e-commerce solutions, and wrote his first book in Germany, *E-Commerce and Online Marketing*, published by Carl Hanser Verlag, Munich. Due to its wide success, he started working as a freelance consultant and author in order to share his experience and knowledge with others. He has written several books for Apress, Hanser, Addison Wesley and other major publishers along with several self-published books—a total of over sixty titles. He also publishes articles in magazines and speaks at major conferences in Germany. Currently, Jörg works as an independent consultant, software developer, and author in Berlin, Germany.

In his occasional spare time, Jörg enjoys reading thrillers and science fiction novels, and going on a round of golf.

Introduction

Node.js is a programming environment based on JavaScript. It's mainly used for web application development, but not restricted to same. In conjunction with the Node Package Manager (npm), it provides a powerful environment to create platform-independent applications.

This book shows the basic parts you need to create a web application. Apart from Node itself, this includes the middleware framework Express and the template language Pug (formerly known as JADE).

The content presents Node in its elementary form, shows the programming of a simple web application, and explains the major modules. In the same style, Express and Pug are explained. The client does not have any particular role in this book. The pages served by the examples are plain HTML.

Foreword

Node.js is one of the most fascinating software environments of recent years. Today it's in version v6.x, a quite mature version. There are two lines: one with Long Term Support (LTS) currently in version 4.x, and the one with the most recent features in version 6.x. The version 6.x has updates quite often, sometimes weekly.

It's necessary to have a well-known language to create web applications instead of inventing just another language all the time. Think of the history of Perl, PHP, Java, Ruby, C in all it derivates, and many more. The final answer might be JavaScript.

The foundation of JavaScript on the server is the V8 engine from Chrome browser that has been extracted and made available as an executable. And it is available on all platforms, finally.

For developers with a strong background in traditional object-oriented languages such as C# or Java, it might sound odd that JavaScript has such a tremendous impact and success. It's a weird mixture of a very simple language and a very rich and quickly expanding ecosystem.

This Book

All codes from the book are available on Github for easy testing and download.

The book is very focused on the first steps and easy examples. There is almost no advanced code and the reference parts contain only those functions required to execute a web application. The purpose is to have all this information handy in one place instead of flipping through hundreds of online sources.

The combination of Node, Express, and Pug is well-tested and the versions used here work together smoothly. There s no support for other software modules and other version combinations.

Who Should Read This Book?

This book is aimed at beginners and web developers who are new to the web world. Node serves mainly the back-end developer. Maybe you are also a web designer, who discovered Node as an excellent way to upgrade your web pages with dynamic elements.

In any case, I tried not to ask any prerequisites or conditions of the reader. You do not need to be a computer scientist, nor in perfect command of language. You don't need to know rocket science. No matter what context you have encountered on Jade, you will be able to read this text.

---

i **What You Need**   In order to understand all examples, you need a working environment for creating web pages. That can be a Windows, a Linux, or even a Mac. It's possible to use any text editor to get the stuff running, but I recommend you use one with a little support while typing the stuff. Check editors such as Visual Studio Code or Sublime Text.

If you have accidentally found this text and cannot do anything with the term "Bootstrap," read it anyway. You will be learning one of the most modern techniques of web development, and the future belongs to the circle of excellent developers who can be build good-looking and device-independent sites.

Examples

You can find the sample project to this book on Github:

- *https://github.com/joergkrause/NodejsExpressPug-Book*

As You Read This Text

I will not dictate how you should read this text. In the first draft of the structure, I have tried several variations and found that there exists no ideal form. However, readers tend today to consume smaller chunks, independent chapters, and focused content. This book addresses this trend by reducing content to small, focused chunks, with no extraneous material.

Beginners should read the text as a narrative from the first to the last page. Those who are already somewhat familiar can safely skip certain sections.

Conventions Used in the Book

The theme is not technically easy to master, because scripts are often too extensive and it would be nice if you could support the best optical reading form. I have therefore included extra line breaks used to aid readability.

In general, each program code is set to a non-proportional font. In addition, scripts have line numbers:

```
1   function send(){
2        // do some stuff here
3   }
```

If you find you need to enter something in the prompt or in a dialog box, this part of the statement is in bold:

```
$ bower install bootstrap
```

The first character is the prompt and is not entered. I use the Linux prompt and the bash shell in the book. The commands will work, without any exception, unchanged even on Windows. The only difference then is the command prompt **C:>** or something similar at the beginning of the line. Usually the instructions are related to relative paths or no paths at all, so the actual prompt shouldn't matter despite the fact that you will be in your working folder.

Expressions and command lines are sometimes peppered with all types of characters, and in almost all cases, it depends on each character. Often, I'll discuss the use of certain characters in precisely such an expression, then the "important" characters with line breaks alone, and also—in this case—line numbers. Line numbers are used to reference the affected symbol in the text exactly (note the : character in line 2):

```
1   a.test {
2     :hover {
3       color: red
4     }
5   }
```

The font is non-proportional, so that the characters are countable and opening and closing parentheses are always among themselves.

Symbols

To facilitate the orientation in the search for a solution, there is a whole range of symbols that are used in the text.

 Tip   This is a tip.

 Information   This is an information.

 Warning   This is a warning.

There are no questionnaires, exercises, or self-tests. It's just a reference, an easy-to-read text to get you on your way.

CHAPTER 1

■ ■ ■

Installation Problems

All instructions, which you find on the Internet about Node, NPM and other modules presuppose one thing: transparent Internet access—which at first sight is worth hardly a mention. Indeed, it represents a problem for many users. Not for the lack of Internet, but for the restrictions in enterprise networks.

Node.Js

Node itself stands as an installation package of choice and can also be installed without the Internet. Since NPM is included, it works just fine online, too. All further components of the application, like Express and Pug, can be installed with *npm*.

Problems with NPM

It's possible that *npm* can't access the Internet the way you expect it. This can be because of missing SSL support or local proxy servers.

Proxy

You can instruct *npm* to use a proxy server:

```
1  npm config set proxy http://proxy.company.com:8080 -g
2  npm config set https-proxy http://proxy.company.com:8080 -g
```

The option *-g* stops the changes globally. Otherwise, it is only valid for the current project and it must be located in the same folder, where a file called *.npmrc* exists. If this is missing, you'll place it there, which is perhaps senseless if you don't plan on using further *npm* commands.

If a username and a password are necessary, it might looks as follows:

```
1  npm config set proxy http://domain%5Cuser:pass@host:port
```

Special characters must become URL encoded here:

- " -> %22
- @ -> %40
- : -> %3A
- \ -> %5C

© Jörg Krause 2017

J. Krause, *Programming Web Applications with Node, Express and Pug*, DOI 10.1007/978-1-4842-2511-0_1

SSL

Access to the Repository is standard. Go around this as follows:

```
1   npm config set strict-ssl false
2   npm config set registry "http://registry.npmjs.org/"
```

Perhaps this combination with the installation procedure can help:

```
1   npm --proxy http://<user>:<pwd>@<proxy>:<port>
2       --without-ssl
3       --insecure
4       -g install <paketname>
```

Problems with Git

Git is needed if you fetch packages via *Bower* or over direct connections from Github. There are two hurdles in enterprise networks:

- A local Proxy is used.

- The protocol *git://* is blocked. (That is a moniker for a special port.)

Many administrators are of the opinion that HTTP and port 80 are enough. However, we developers want more. Thus, Git must be configured accordingly.

You receive the local Git installation under Linux as follows:

$ sudo apt-get install git

Under Windows you should use an installer, which can also bring along a Shell, which contains a part of the *not-local* function. One does not have to switch a lot mentally, and can invariably use most Linux commands this way.

Here you find the suitable package: *https://git-scm.com/download/win* Configure the options as shown on the following screens:

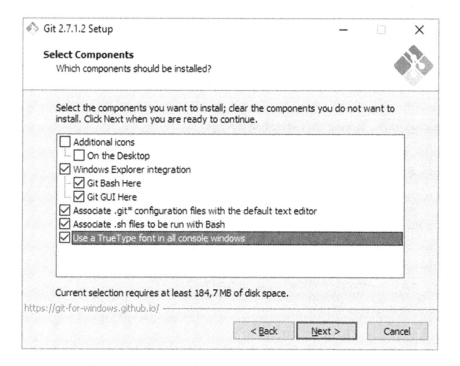

Figure 1-1. *Installation options*

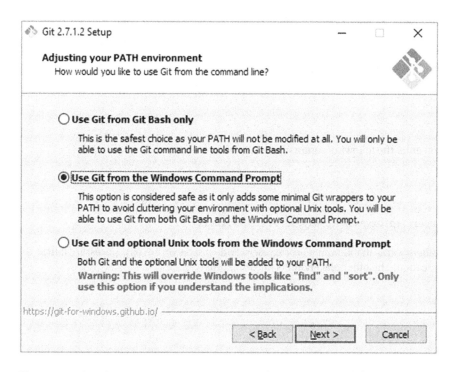

Figure 1-2. *Starting options*

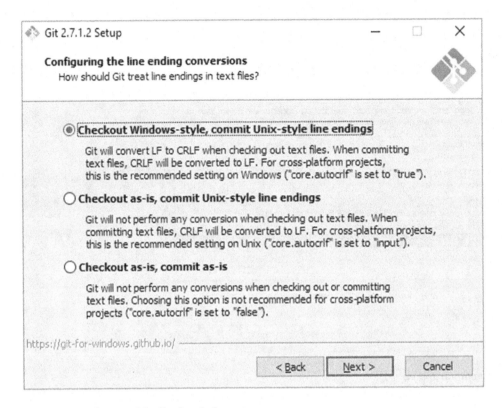

Figure 1-3. *Behavior of the line break characters*

Leave all other options unchanged.

The installation for Windows comprehensively has *no* graphic surface. This must be procured separately. In the long run, however, the command line is the better and faster way.

Proxy

In order to use a proxy, you enter the following command (in a line):

```
1  git config
2      --global
3      http.proxy
4      http://<proxyuser>:<proxypwd>@<proxy.server.com>:<port>
```

Replace the place holders with suitable values. *<proxyuser>* and *<proxywd>* are only necessary if the Proxy requires an authentication. The other placeholders mark the proxy.

Git protocols

With the following command (again in a line) you can switch to *https*:

```
1   git config
2       --global
3       url."https://<username>@".insteadOf git://
```

The placeholder *<username>* marks a private Repository in Git. The quotation marks protect the name in the case of blanks:

You can omit the value for the glocal access completely and instead use Github:

```
1   git config
2       --global
3       url.https://github.com/.insteadOf git://
```

Online installation

Even if the information of a proxy is not sufficient, the online access remains. The classic way thereby exists in downloading an installation package and the local installation. For Windows users, those are the MSI packages; for Linux users, it's usually DEB packages (Debian, Ubuntu, Mint, etc.) or RPM packages (Suse, Fedora, RedHat, etc.).

However, NPM packages are not part of package collections, but instructions over source and dependence. With the installation, the specified fragments from the Internet are downloaded.

Preparation

The dependence of an Internet connection can't fundamentally be absolutely avoided. But it is sufficient to have "other" machines with Internet access. They can use a detour. That can be done for individual packages anyway, but many packages have dozens of hundreds of dependences, sometimes over several stages. Here it is meaningful to have something automatic.

The solution is the package *npmbox*. It consists of two command line tools: *npmbox* for downloading and packing, and *npmunbox* for unpacking. If you can receive brief access to the Internet on the search machine, install *npmbox* there. It simplifies handling substantially. Even if that cannot be done, you find more instructions for *hard cases* below.

First you install *npmbox* on the source machine with Internet access:

```
npm install npmbox -g
```

In order to check if it worked, you enter the following command:

```
npmbox --help
```

You receive a quick guide of a very simple tool.

Hard cases

So that you can access *npmbox* on the desired machine, you must package it yourself. That is a kind of recursive approach—*npmbox* packs itself:

```
npmbox npmbox
```

5

The result is a file with the file extension *.npmbox*.

Copy the file on the desired machine. The package is a so-called tarball. *npm* can directly go around Tar und usually needs no other software. If you packed something before with *npmbox*, you need *npmunbox* for unpacking.

Access to Tar

Tarball

Tar is an archives software. The name comes from "Tape of archives" (archiving on tape drive). In order to store data on volumes, one combines many small files into a large file. Contrary to ZIP, TAR is a pure combination method, which does thereby becomes a compressed file. The format receives the original meta data of the files, such as rights and link information. You can find more on Wikipedia:

`https://en.wikipedia.org/wiki/Tar_(computing)`

On Linux, *tar* is a standard device which is always available.

tar -xvf yourfile.tar

On Windows, there are several options. To the standard environments, which are used in Node installations, Git shall be included. Git is available at first as described, but also as MSI. The installer comes with a rudimentary BASH Shell. This cannot do everything as under Linux, but it can use *tar*. Open Bash Shell under Windows and then use the same command:

$tar -xvf yourfile.tar

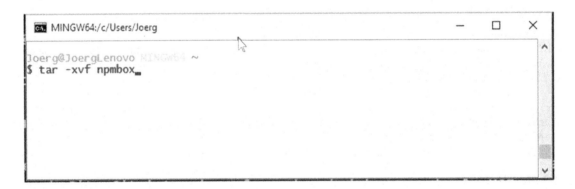

Figure 1-4. *Bash with tar command on Windows*

If that does not fit, well-known archive programs like 7-Zip are suitable too.

Installing NpmBox

After the command is implemented, all files are in the folder *.npmbox-cache.*

 If you unpack several packages, all this will be copied into the same folder. That is because there can be repetitions by dependence.

Now it's *npm*'s turn (in a line):

```
1    npm install --global
2                    --cache ./.npmbox-cache
3                    --optional
4                    --cache-min 999999
5                    --fetch-retries 0
6                    --fetch-retry-factor 0
7                    --fetch-retry-mintimeout 1
8                    --fetch-retry-maxtimeout 2
9    npmbox
```

\ or /   Under Linux you always use the information of a path, like /. Under Windows, you use \.

However, if you use the Git Bash under windows, then \ also works. Under Windows 10, it works with *cmd.exe* and /, but with some problems, like no longer having a functioning TAB key.

The last line contains the actual package. The option '–cache' is there to determine that *npm* won't access the Repository, but the local folder. Often a short version is enough:

npm i -cache ./.npmbox-cache

Installing Packages

Now this pedantic *npm* command isn't quite what developers want to type frequently. Therefore, *npmunbox* exists. This is a future device for the command line, which simplifies the unpacking procedure.

npmunbox <packagename>

As package name <packagename> you use the name, which was also used during the package procedure.

If there's a problem, the *npmbox* version of the source machine most likely doesn't match the one on the desired machine. Check that carefully, before you go further.

---

npmunbox has a few more options, since a part of the behavior of *npm* must be simulated here:

- -v, -verbose: Show *npm* expenditures (standard).

- -s, -silent: Additional expenditures are suppressed.

- -g, -global: Install packages globally (in the path, not in the protect folder).

- -C, -prefix: The switch 'npm –prefix' shows the standard listing.

- -S, -save: The switch 'npm –save' is stored in *package.json* in *dependencies*.

- -D, -save-dev: The switch 'npm –save dev' is stored in *package.json* in *devDependencies*.

- -O, -save-optional: The switch 'npm –save-optional' is stored in *package.json* in *optionalDependencies*.

- -E, -save-exact: The switch 'npm –save exact' leads to versions in the SemVer format being placed with the exact number.

CHAPTER 2

■ ■ ■

The Components of an Application

MEAN stands for MongoDb, Express, AngularJS and Node. Node is the basis of the stack. Express supplies a comfortable entrance to HTTP. AngularJS serves the client with the help of an MVC Pattern (Model View Controller). MongoDB is a document-oriented NoSQL database, which can deal directly with JSON data. Everything together illustrates a complete server and client page environment on the basis of JavaScript. Certainly, there's way more to it in practice:

- HTML as a basis for *CSS*, at best in a group with a preprocessor such as LESS and a CSS Framework such as Bootstrap

- a design template as a basis for more complex controls (usually a Bootstrap theme)

- extension libraries for the server (via **npm**) and the client (via Bower**)**

The Package Manager

In the JavaScript world, several package managers have been developed. But why are such additional tools needed at all? Wikipedia has the following answer for this:

> *A package management software makes the comfortable administration possible of software, which is present in complex program form or on an operating system. In addition installing, updating and deinstallation.*

A package management always consists of a Repository and a client. In some cases the Repository is only the source of the description, not contents. One uses in the JavaScript world:

- **npm**, that is, the Node package manager. It comes along automatically, if Node is installed. All server page packages are called up and installed over Npm. Npm can also supply further tools. Npm serves also to install the package manager for the client packages, Bower:

- **Bower** administers client page Frameworks and libraries. Bower even administers no data, but only descriptions. The packages are called up over **Git** from **GitHub**. As such, it is guaranteed that the most current versions are there and the developers of the libraries for the distribution on various Repositories don't have to care about that themselves.

© Jörg Krause 2017
J. Krause, *Programming Web Applications with Node, Express and Pug*, DOI 10.1007/978-1-4842-2511-0_2

Windows Repositories for client libraries   Git brings along a simple GUI and command line tools. Whoever works with Powershell should take a look at **Chocolatey**. This project brings the JavaScript world together with the Windows world. Here you work with the original tools, since this is more transparent and direct. Chocolatey simplifies some things, covered in addition to the connections, which is rather obstructive when learning.

Libraries and Frameworks

Libraries offer a set of elementary functions. Jquery, for example, allows the manipulation of DOM elements. However, Frameworks offer certain functions and a pattern for complete applications.

AngularJS realizes the client page MVC Pattern and places bidirectional data connection (apart from many other functions). Surely there are intersections between both and the demarcation is often not so clear, but it makes it more simple to meet a selection. Several (many) libraries often co-exist, while you should choose only one Framework. While keeping a close watch, we should also see that web applications are split—in client and server. Thus, it is necessary to find an amount of libraries and (!) a Framework for the client and then again with the server.

Basis Libraries of the Server

In this book series a form of the MEAN stack is presented. MEAN stands for:

- MongoDB/MySQL
- Express
- AngularJS
- Node

That is striking, but only the half truth. The choice of the database is often not primary and most components are often not sufficient in order to illustrate the entire Web stack. It should be considered for the server, that:

- As server page, Routing Framework and **Express** middleware is used. It supplies the Routing functions and is an efficient application framework.
- As Template library, **Pug** is used, which takes over the production of the HTML forms instead of Razor, as far as this takes place on the server.

Client Page Libraries

Thus we can deliver web pages and make services available. The client support remains:

- **AngularJS** as the comprehensive framework for the structuring of the pages
- **Bootstrap** as design and style framework
- **jQuery** as implicitly library used by Bootstrap for the access to the Document Object Model (DOM)

All of this would also be used in the ASP.NET world. Here .NET offers no direct entrance, because the client can be served only over JavaScript.

Unit Tests

JavaScript as an underlying language is comparatively weak. Also, with the detour over TypeScript or the new functions in ES 6, the depth and accuracy of the code monitoring of a compilor language are not on the same level as with Java or C#. Therefore, a still greater importance is attached to unit tests:

Principles

The way Web applications are developed has changed a lot in the recent years. Dynamic elements in the browser are normal and the running of complete applications in JavaScript is frequently used. The browser becomes a kind of mini–operating system, which avails itself in the net of various data sources—the services of our servers.

Web Apps

Applications are called Web Apps if they exist directly in the browser and communicate only with the server in order to reload data dynamically. The server thereby first delivers the app and then supports it by services, for example to the access of a database. The server places thereby a so called API (Application Programming Interface) as available. Usually this is based on JSON.

Web sites

Most web sites are rather classically programmed. That means the detectability of contents through search engines, extremely short load times, and simple structure. The server produces finished HTML and all dynamic elements by manipulating the HTML with the help of small scripts. Forms are used for interaction and the indicator functions by the server steered. Web sites are then supported by JavaScript so that they appear interactive, which is necessary in order to appear modern and functional.

However, this approach is problematic for several reasons. They must hold two code environments separately from each other: on the one hand for the browser, on the other hand for the server. Both worlds are closely connected. Changes on one page can release errors on the other page. This entwinement is critical and hardly permanently controllable.

Stateless HTML

If Web Apps are not an option (complex, slow, not a search engine suite) and also not web sites (maintenance-unfriendly, faulted), then it is time to think about a new strategy. This is where Node comes in, because the separation of the code environments is by far less drastic, if the same programming language is used. Additionally, a certain programming style should be used. This is so-called stateless HTML.

Stateless HTML is a piece of HTML that is always identical to the condition of the web site and independent. Whether the user is registered or not, whether it is morning or afternoon, it is all the same. No matter which geographical place was used, the HTML of the page is always alike. Thus a significant part of maintenance cost is lost. Parts of the page, which are dependent on the user or action, do not become part of the HTML. They are procured like a Web App by services and provided dynamically. Thus, simple loading from HTML pages is in Node, as in the examples shown.

Imagine a page with contents, which readers can discuss. The contents part is for all users directly. Also, each search engine sees the same contents. This part is static and condition-independent. That does not mean that the articles must lie statically on the hard disk. They can be assembled on the server from a database. It is part of the panel and completely dynamic against it. Each user sees his own contributions differently and has perhaps personalized the representations. This part is provided and delivered differently.

The approach does not only simplify programming. It also increases the performance clearly. The less dynamic portion is easier to process on the server and on the client. A cache can be used comprehensively and be further relieved from the server. Also, in the event of an error delivering of static pages, it is more robust and more reliable. The omission of the dynamic functions is annoying, but the page remains complete and searchable. However, an improvement of the user experience is crucial.

The User Experience

Modern Web applications are complex. There is a user login, account administration, carts, evaluation systems, and much more. Each of these functions consists of HTML pages, which supply the primary organization. Typical pages look as follows:

```
1   <!DOCTYPE html>
2   <html>
3
4   <head>
5       <meta charset="utf-8">
6       <title>File Manager</title>
7       <link rel="stylesheet" href="style.css">
8       <script defer src="app.js"></script>
9   </head>
10
11  <body>
12      <nav>
13          <a href="/">Home</a>
14          <a href="/show">Files</a>
15          <a href="/upload">Upload</a>
16          <div class="account-menu">
17              <!-- Dynamic Part -->
18          </div>
19      </nav>
20
21      <section id="main">
22          <!-- This is where your content goes -->
23          <h1>Welcome to our File Manager</h1>
24          Manage your files online.
25      </section>
26
27      <footer>
28          Copyright &copy; 2016
29      </footer>
30  </body>
31
32  </html>
```

This page loads extremely quickly and represents contents immediately. Then, the application script *app.js* is loaded and settles some things dynamically:

- checks by means of Cookie and AJAX whether the user is registered

- loads the dynamic menu for the user

- configures static contents dynamically

The first two points are obvious. The latter is somewhat subtler. Naturally, nobody wants to provide the same HTML again and again for many content pages. Here you could proceed differently. Use JavaScript in order to call static contents up from the server. In addition, all links which load pages and use the same layout are intercepted by JavaScript and the site, as it is loaded from the server. Contents are extracted, namely the part which is located in the main section '<section id="main">'. This part is then exchanged. The advantage consists of the fact that the static HTML is unchanged. It does not depend on a situation. Thus, application at complexity is less. Nevertheless, the user has the soft load behavior of an AJAX-driven application. If you still adapt the History in the browser of the page now, it is nearly perfect (with the API of the browser).

Summary

With the organization and structuring of a Node application you must first know what you want to build—a Web app or a web site.

With a Web app, you concentrate on Frameworks such as AngularJS. Node supplies the app as collection from an HTML page and some to JavaScript files. A variety of support services makes it possible for the app to communicate with the server.

With a web site, it is better to only use jQuery and to add somewhat smart JavaScript elements dynamically. Node supplies static HTML pages and some support services.

CHAPTER 3

Introduction to Node

Node.js is an Open Source Platform which is used for the server page execution of JavaScript. The core of Node.js forms the in C/C++ written and therefore fast JavaScript implementation V8, which compiles the JavaScript code before the execution in native machine code.

Besides that, Node.js covers integrated modules, e.g., the HTTP module, in order to host a web server. Further modules can be installed with the 'every day used' **npm** package manager.

The asynchronous architecture of JavaScript makes a parallel processing of, for example, Client connections or database accesses.

With Node.js (short: Node), it's possible to provide high-performance network and particularly Web applications, which can communicate with the Web browser (with the assistance of a WebSocket connection) even in real time. Since modern Web browsers—just like Node—use JavaScript, code can be delivered to both sides and partly used together. However, it is important to note, that now you must only know one programming language in order to provide the entire Web application.

Elementary in JavaScript

This text assumes that you can read JavaScript halfway fluently. Even if this is the case, it can be that some examples are nevertheless more complex. Usually it is because of callback methods that the code appears unclear.

Read the following example attentively:

```
1  function action(v) {
2    console.log(v);
3  }
4
5  function execute(value, callback) {
6    callback(value);
7  }
8
9  execute("Hallo Node", action);
```

Here, a function is agreed upon (line 1) which later (line 9) is used as a callback function of the actual work function (line 5). Thus, functions can be agreed upon, basically implementing options. This is very often used in Node, e.g., with evaluating a request, where the callback takes place, if the request was received, and the method parameter reached via the request values.

Since JavaScript has in each case only one thread it is different than in other programming languages) the use of asynchronous procedures is enormously important. Otherwise, a call could block all the following calls. Asynchrony becomes controllable by the use of callback functions.

© Jörg Krause 2017
J. Krause, *Programming Web Applications with Node, Express and Pug*, DOI 10.1007/978-1-4842-2511-0_3

Installation and Configuration

This section shows the basic configuration and the structure of a first Node environment. That also includes the use of the package manager.

Configuration in package.json

Every Node application contains a file with the name *package.json*. Thus, the project can be configured. The file extensions that it concerns are an object in the JSON style. JSON stands for *JavaScript Object Notation* and can be simply processed by JavaScript.

Here is an example of how such a file can look:

```
 1   {
 2     "name": "book-exampleproject",
 3     "version": "1.0.0",
 4     "description": "This is a project with book examples.",
 5     "main": "server.js",
 6     "repository": {
 7       "type": "git",
 8       "url": "https://github.com/joergisageek/nodejs-samples"
 9     },
10     "dependencies": {
11       "express": "latest",
12       "mongoose": "latest"
13     },
14     "author": "Joerg Krause",
15     "license": "MIT",
16     "homepage": "http://www.joergkrause.de"
17   }
```

Pay attention to subordinated objects, such as *dependencies* or *repository*. In each case, the name of the features can be seen on the left; on the right, the data. These can also be objects. This goes on until scalar types are used, like character strings or numbers.

Actually, not everything is needed here. The simplest file could also look as follows:

```
1   {
2     "name": "book-exampleproject",
3     "main": "server.js"
4   }
```

Thus the project has a name and it has a starting file—the re-entry point for the JavaScript interpreter. With *server.js* the processing of the project begins.

Initialize the Node Application

The following section first shows how you make the structure of the application on the command line of a Linux system. In the inspection examples, and for making the screen photos, Ubuntu was used. However, it should require for every *nix-system a comparable operational sequence.

Subsequently, the most important steps for a Windows system and a Visual Studio 2015 are shown.

Approach under Linux

As already described, Node starts the application over the instructions in the file *package.json*. So that nothing runs wrongly, there is an **npm** command that creates the file **npm init**. In order to start with a new Node application, you need to proceed as follows:

1. Produce a folder: `mkdir book-project`.

2. Change into this folder: `cd book-project`.

3. Initialize the project: `npm init`.

You can leave the interactively queried parameters unchanged the first time. Designate only the starting file in *server.js*. The Node application is now ready for launch—even if not much meaningful happens yet—and can be started.

Start a Node Application

In principle, the start takes place via call of the executable file **node** (Linux) and/or **node.exe** (Windows). The script runs and ends immediately again. The program is terminated. If it is to run permanently, this must be programmed in *server.js* accordingly. If the script runs and you want to terminate it on the command line, use the key combination 'CTRL + C'. In practice, as already described, you'll use **npm** for the start if you are using Linux. Under Windows with Visual Studio *F5*, (Debug ➤ Start Debugging) is the simplest way to start locally.

Automatic Restart

When it comes to changes, these should be examined as simply as possible. Thus the program must be first stopped and started again—what a annoying procedure! However, that can be automated, as changes at a file are supervised.

The **npm** package *nodemon* supplies this function. Install this first globally:

```
npm install -g nodemon
```

Then, don't start with 'node', but with 'nodemon':

```
nodemon server.js
node server.js
```

Alternatively, **npm** can be used in the current folder:

```
npm start
```

Since at this moment *server.js* does not exist, an error message will occur.

 'npm start' versus 'node server.js'   !> When a starting script is agreed upon in the file *package.*

json, then you can start it with **npm start**. If no starting script exists, then Node implements internally *node server.js. server.js* is here the exemplarily used application script. The starting script is important (in order to settle actions before the execution) as an example to translate LESS files in CSS or for transpiling TypeScript into JavaScript. To that extent, you're always on the safe side with **npm start**.

Approach under Windows

This section presupposes that you installed Visual Studio 2015. Most functions for Node and the accesses to the Repositories are already finished and/or present.

⚠ **Path length**   The functions with Visual Studio are very simple and comfortable. Above all, the Debugger is a genuine assistance. Unfortunately, Windows still has a delimitation of the path length on 260 characters. Many under Linux-provided packages use deep path structures. You should start with a master path like *D:\ Apps* or *C:\Dev* and in no case with the default path of Visual Studio, which is already about 100 characters. Keep the project names as short as possible.

A new simple Node project is produced with the *Blank Node.js Web Application*.

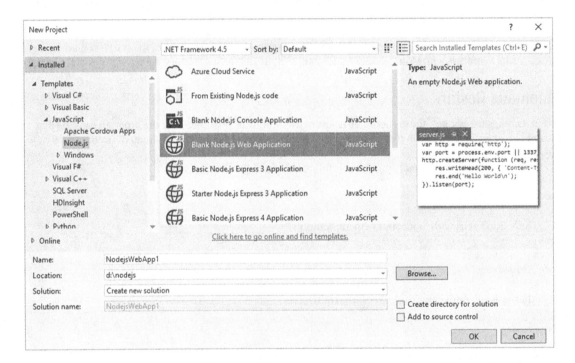

Figure 3-1. *Node.js Project template*

As already described, Node starts the application over the instructions in the file *package.json*. This file is already present in the new project. As a starting file you should use *server.js*. The Node application is now already ready to launch—even if not much happens yet—and can be started. As always, simply press *F5*. Node starts in a console and the browsers open with the output "Hello World". This output was produced by the project template.

In the further process of the text, the procedure for Visual Studio is not shown each time, but uses the command line version for Linux. The differences are small and in the following table summarized.

Table 3-1. *Differences Linux/Windows*

Action	Linux	Windows+VS 2015
Start	npm start	F5
Install package	npm install pkg	Context menu in folder 'npm': *Install new Package*

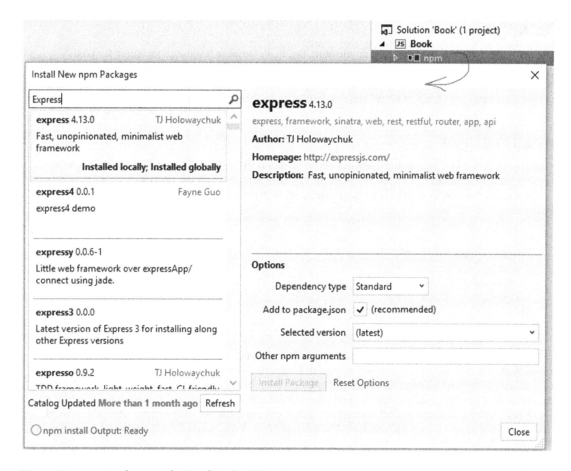

Figure 3-2. *npm packages with Visual Studio 2015*

The first Application

The first application should be particularly simple. The simplest version of the *package.json* file looks as follows:

```
1  {
2    "name": "book-project",
3    "main": "server.js"
4  }
```

Since this configuration refers to *server.js*, this script will be provided next. So that you see the fact that it functions, it should only produce expenditures by the means of 'console.log'.

```
1   console.log('Our first node-Applikation');
```

Start the application as described before.

Packages

Packages extend the functionality of an application. But that's because Node isn't just there for Web applications, but also operating system–independent programs and thus server page functions. Also, for a simple project additional packages are needed. Node is very slim and modular. Since Node is has package management **npm** connected, both programs are used for both use and administration.

Install Packages

In the configuration file *package.json* dependence of further packages is defined, besides to the application, of course. You can enter the packages manually or leave this to the installation process.

Here is an example, in which the package "Express" with the version "4.8.6" is defined as an additional dependence.

```
1   {
2     "name": "book-project",
3     "main": "server.js",
4     "dependencies": {
5     "express": "~4.8.6"
6     }
7   }
```

The version number was introduced with a tilde '~'. This procedure—the tilde is only one of many possibilities—for its versions serves to strengthen its semantic information. Packages are developed very fast, and with many dependencies it can be difficult to remain both current and operator-safe. The tilde ensures the fact that the most current version in the subordinated cycle is used. The version of the third stage may change, but the second one not. If a package with the version 4.8.7 or 4.8.9 appears, then this is used. However, if 4.9.0 appears, then it is not used. The untested transferred to such a released would be too risky.

ℹ **Versions**   Versions are indicated in four stages: major, minor, patch, build. The fourth example is

"Express," a main version number which stands stable for a long time and only changes for specific reasons. 8 is the current development cycle. 6 is the patch level. Corrections and smaller adjustments will appear here. The build number is often used only internally and is not distributed at package administrations.

A further method is the installation of packages over the command line—concretely the command line tool (or Command Line Interface, cli)—**npm**. Usually this is faster and simpler. You must only decide whether the package is made available only locally for only one application or globally for all future projects.

The command reads:

```
npm install <PaketName> --save
```

Follow the command in the folder of the application and use the option '-save', then the entry in the file *package.json* will appear automatically. The package (thus, the files of which it consists) is put down in a folder with the name *node_modules*.

Now it can occur that you have packages in the file *package.json*, which are not currently installed. The call of the Repository must still take place. In addition it is sufficient to call the folder, in which the file *package.json* lies, and do the following:

```
npm install
```

Dependence on further packages dissolves the command itself.

If several pages are to be installed, then these can be indicated in a command (here: *express, mongoose* and *pass*):

```
npm install express mongoose passport --save
```

The complete installation of an environment for developing in Node thus only needs a few commands:

1. npm init initializes a standard environment

2. package.json configures this environment

3. npm install loads the necessary packages

Provide a Server Application

Node is a server application. This must be started, so that requests are implemented to be worked on and able to take actions. While with Node very much can be programmed—up to desktop applications—the application of standards is a Web application. There is therefore a library, which takes over basic tasks of a Web application Express. Most examples, which you find on platforms such as Stackoverflow[1], use Express.

Q More about Express   Express itself has its own chapter. In the appendix you can find a command overview in addition.

However, the first step in Node should take place without Express, in order to see the simplest example possible. This introduction text emulates consciously some functions of Express, in order to make the totally enclosed functionality understandable.

---

[1] http://www.stackoverflow.com

The simplest Server

Basis of the application are three files:

- package.json
- server.js
- index.html

package.json was already regarded—this configures the application. *server.js* is the active re-entry point—there the script starts. *index.html* is a static HTML page, which is exemplarily delivered here.

File: package.json

```
1   {
2       "name": "http-server",
3       "main": "server.js"
4   }
```

File: index.html

```
1    <!DOCTYPE html>
2    <html lang="en">
3    <head>
4    <meta charset="UTF-8">
5    <title>The first page</title>
6    <style>
7    body {
8        text-align:center;
9        background:#EFEFEF;
10       padding-top:50px;
11   }
12   </style>
13   </head>
14     <body>
15
16     <h1>Hello Node!</h1>
17
18     </body>
19     </html>
```

The file *server.js* supplies the active part:

File: server.js

```
1    var http = require('http');
2    var fs = require('fs');
3    var port = process.env.port || 1337;
4
5    http.createServer(function (req, res) {
6      console.log("Anforderung auf Port 1337")
7      res.writeHead(200, {
8        'Content-Type': 'text/html',
9        'Access-Control-Allow-Origin': '*'
10     });
```

```
11    var read = fs.createReadStream(__dirname + '/index.html');
12    read.pipe(res);
13  }).listen(port);
```

Here, the first two components from Node are used: "http" and "fs". The module "http" serves to program HTTP communication. With "fs" (File System), the access of a file system becomes possible. Therefore, everything is present which needs this program. The file *index.html* can be read and sent.

Now start the project just as previously. If now, with the help of the browser, a call of the agreed-upon address *http://localhost:1337* takes place, the example page appears and on the console the output "requirement on port 1337" appears.

ⓘ Port The port was here completely arbitrarily specified. There is no deeper meaning behind 1337. Take a free port more largely to 1000 for the first tests.

A Server with Express

Why Express has such outstanding importance is shown by the following example. It fulfills the same task with the same example file:

server.js with Express 4

```
1    var http = require('http');
2    var express = require('express');
3    var path = require('path');
4
5    var port = process.env.port || 1337;
6    var app = express();
7
8    app.get('/', function (req, res) {
9        res.sendFile(path.join(__dirname, '/index.html'));
10   });
11
12   app.listen(port);
13   console.log('Request with Express on Port 1337.');
```

For this to function, Express has to be installed first:

```
npm install express --save
```

The advantage here is the abstraction of the HTTP level. You do not have to argue about the intricacies of protocols anymore. You do not have to worry about features of file access either.

Handling Requests

As the example with *Express* already showed, it mostly revolves around the processing of a specific URL and the determination suitable for such an action. This can take place directly with Node. In the beginning, it is meaningful to understand the mechanism behind it and to go on without complex modules.

Introduction to Routing

The process of passing on is generally called "Routing." The URL is the "Route." You will in practice always define several of such routes and give those callbacks, which are named with the suitable URL by which a request takes place. In addition, routes are connected with HTTP verbs, thus the commands possible in HTTP such as GET or POST.

Node makes the function "url.parse" available, in order to determine the components of a URL. In addition, one must certainly know these. The following illustration explains it:

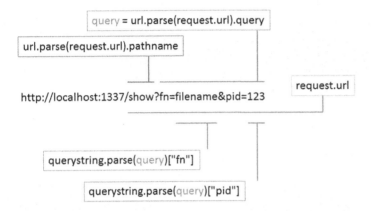

Figure 3-3. *Components of a URL*

In addition, the server is somewhat differently structured—indeed, as an independent module. You should make that very early, because JavaScript applications become very unclear very fast. The module in this example is called *start.js*:

Listing 3-1. Simple Server start.js

```
1   var http = require("http");
2   var url = require("url");
3
4   function start() {
5
6     console.log("Starting.");
7
8     function onRequest(request, response) {
9       var pathname = url.parse(request.url).pathname;
10      console.log("Request for path " + pathname + " received.");
11      response.writeHead(200, {
12        "Content-Type": "text/plain"
13      });
14      response.write("The first Server");
15      response.end();
16    }
17
```

```
18    var port = process.env.port || 1337;
19    http.createServer(onRequest).listen(port);
20    console.log("Has been started.");
21
22  }
23
24  exports.start = start;
```

Modules are made available over the global instruction "exports." The internal and the external name do not have to agree. However, it facilitates the maintenance to do this. The file *server.js* now looks as follows:

*File: *server.js*

```
1    var server = require('./start');
2
3    server.start();
```

```
> webapps@1.0.0 start C:\Apps\books\ne7
> node server.js

Starting.
Has been startet.
Request for / received.
Request for /favicon.ico received.
```

```
┌────────────────────────────────────┐
│ ⌂ localhost:1337        ×  ╲        │
├────────────────────────────────────┤
│ ← → C  ① localhost:1337            │
├────────────────────────────────────┤
│  The first Server                   │
└────────────────────────────────────┘
```

Figure 3-4. *The Server recognizes the Paths*

The application is now able to extract the path from the URL of the requesting Client. This is the starting point of the Routing. Typical routes are then:

- /index
- /logon
- /logoff
- /show
- /show?fn=filename

Now, it is not particularly smart to pack the router logic into the server. Quickly, the logic becomes more complex and then the code very difficult. You also get a better feeling for the way such a router works if you separate the router function.

Create a new JavaScript file with the name *router.js*. This looks as follows:

File: router.js

```
1    function route(pathname) {
2      console.log("Route for path requested: " + pathname);
3    }
4    exports.route = route;
```

This script still contains no functionality. However, first the connection with the first script is to be manufactured. The connection can be made directly or by draws to coupling. As a draft sample, Dependency Injection is used. A procedure with which the caller dependence can be called is injected from the outside.

ⓘ Dependency Injection   Read more about coupled architectures in the article by Martin Fowler that can be found here: *http://martinfowler.com/articles/injection.html*.

Now the new server function, the file *server.js*:

File: server.js

```
1   var server = require('./start');
2   var router = require('./router');
3
4   server.start(router);
```

The file *start.js*, which contains the application core, is still unchanged to a large extent. The new router function is only called, however it still does nothing meaningful except the console output.

Listing 3-2. start.js with Router

```
1   var http = require("http");
2   var url = require("url");
3
4   function start(router) {
5
6     console.log("Startet.");
7
8     function onRequest(request, response) {
9       var pathname = url.parse(request.url).pathname;
10      router.route(pathname);
11      response.writeHead(200, {
12        "Content-Type": "text/plain"
13      });
14      response.write("The first Server");
15      response.end();
16    }
17
18    var port = process.env.port || 1337;
19    http.createServer(onRequest).listen(port);
20    console.log("Was started.");
21
22  }
23
24  exports.start = start;
```

The calls of "require" then look for a suitable module and/or for a file with the indicated name. The exported names can then be called.

That access to "exports" in the previous script is based on a global module, which always makes Node available.

The function *onRequest* is hidden in the starting function, so that it remains private. It is then handed over as a callback function to the method "createServer". If a request arrives, Node will call the method *onRequest*, in order to begin processing.

Now the application can be started.

Architecture of the Application

Since now different actions for different routes are to be settled, the provided ones must be filled with the necessary logic. As a simple example, the call of a list of files (route */show*) and the possibility are suitable to uploading files (route */upload*). In addition, the first three methods are provided, which concern the execution:

- home: the homepage
- show: show the file list and download process of a file
- upload: upload a file

Also, this part is made available as separate module.

File: handlers.js

```
1   function home() {
2      console.log("Request 'home' called.");
3   }
4   function show() {
5      console.log("Request 'show' called.");
6   }
7   function upload() {
8      console.log("Request 'upload' called.");
9   }
10  exports.home = home;
11  exports.show = show;
12  exports.upload = upload;
```

The router now gets access to these functions, in order to take action when the route is called. So that the allocation is flexible, the routes are connected with processors over a JavaScript object.

File: server.js

```
1   var server = require("./start");
2   var router = require("./router");
3   var requestHandlers = require("./handlers");
4
5   var handler = {};
6   handler["/"] = requestHandlers.home;
7   handler["/show"] = requestHandlers.show;
8   handler["/upload"] = requestHandlers.upload;
9
10  server.start(router.route, handler);
```

Now if the path is recognized (which originates from the list of the routes), the appropriate method is called. Action and execution are separate. What develops here is by way a kind of middleware (called the Framework), that is most frequently set under Node, but also *Express Middleware*. If the path */show* is thus recognized, the function *show()* in *requestHandlers* is called.

Now the actual functionality can be implemented. Node has some reloadable modules, which supply the suitable functions

File: start.js

```
1   var http = require("http");
2   var url = require("url");
3
4   function start(route, handler) {
5     function onRequest(request, response) {
6       var pathname = url.parse(request.url).pathname;
7       if (route(pathname, handler)) {
8         response.writeHead(200, {
9           "Content-Type": "text/plain"
10        });
11        response.write("Hello Router");
12        response.end();
13      } else {
14        response.writeHead(404, {
15          "Content-Type": "text/plain"
16        });
17        response.write("404 Not found");
18        response.end();
19      }
20    }
21    var port = process.env.port || 1337;
22    http.createServer(onRequest).listen(port);
23    console.log("Server started.");
24  }
25
26  exports.start = start;
```

In this script, depending on each call the path will either be handled by the router and then send the regular answer with the HTTP status code 200 or it becomes—if the route was not recognized—the status code 404.

Now *router.js* extends. The call of the methods of the business logic now happens dynamically and it already exists in elementary error handling.

File: router.js

```
1   function route(pathname, handler) {
2     console.log("Request for " + pathname);
3     if (typeof handler[pathname] === 'function') {
4       handler[pathname]();
5       return true;
6     } else {
7       console.log("No Method found for " + pathname);
8       return null;
9     }
10  }
11  exports.route = route;
```

Here it will first be seen (line 3), whether a callback function for the appropriate path exists or not. JavaScript returns "undefined" if this is not the case, so that if this is not the case the "else" branch is implemented. If the function exists, it is called (line 4). The function can return something (which must still be implemented) and this return value is handed over later to the server and then sent to the client. Here only 'true' is returned, in order to show to the server that everything is correct.

```
> simplerouter@1.0.0 start C:\Apps\books\ne7\SimpleRouter
> node server.js

Server started.
Request for /
Request 'home' called.
Request for /favicon.ico
No Method found for /favicon.ico
Request for /home
No Method found for /home
Request for /show
Request 'show' called.
```

Figure 3-5. *Reaction to different Routes*

Now you must create the actual functions of the business logic. In addition this must return something, because instead of the static text an output will take place in HTML to the browser.

The third version of the file *start.js* now shows how this works:

File: start.js

```
1    var http = require("http");
2    var url = require("url");
3
4    function start(route, handler) {
5      function onRequest(request, response) {
6        var pathname = url.parse(request.url).pathname;
7        var content = route(pathname, handler);
8        if (content) {
9          response.writeHead(200, {
10            "Content-Type": "text/plain"
11          });
12          response.write(content);
13          response.end();
14        } else {
15          response.writeHead(404, {
16            "Content-Type": "text/plain"
17          });
18          response.write("404 Not found");
19          response.end();
20        }
21      }
22      var port = process.env.port || 1337;
23      http.createServer(onRequest).listen(port);
24      console.log("Server started.");
25    }
26
27    exports.start = start;
```

If the middleware functions now return HTML, Node will output this as soon as the suitable path is called. The delivery takes place in line 10, the output at the client at line 12.

The router now gives the values of the called logic functions back (line 4):

Datei: File.js

```
1   function route(pathname, handler) {
2     console.log("Request for " + pathname);
3     if (typeof handler[pathname] === 'function') {
4       return handler[pathname]();
5     } else {
6       console.log("No Method found for " + pathname);
7       return null;
8     }
9   }
10  exports.route = route;
```

The business logic in *handler.js* should return something now instead of the expenditures to the browser invisible console:

File: handlers.js

```
1   function home() {
2     return "Request 'home' called.";
3   }
4   function show() {
5     return "Request 'show' called.";
6   }
7   function upload() {
8     return "Request 'upload' called.";
9   }
10  exports.home = home;
11  exports.show = show;
12  exports.upload = upload;
```

So far, this functions and can be used. However, in the example we work with files. This can be problematic if the operations last for a while. Node is like each JavaScript implementation is single-threaded; thus, in each case only one request can be worked on. During high reading, this can lead to a bottleneck. Requirements should therefore always be treated asynchronously. While the server on the hard disk looks with the help of the operating system for files, Node can work on further requirements. Certainly, the file function must return to it immediately and a further callback function is necessary.

Synchronous and Asynchronous Calls

One differentiates here between synchronous and asynchronous calls. Synchronous calls do not block Node. Asynchronous, however, do. It is "best practice" in JavaScript to always program asynchronously.

The example uses file access functions, which Node makes available over the module "fs" (File System). The functions are asynchronous according to standard and, only if necessary, also synchronously usable.

Excerpt of handlers.js (synchronously)

```
1    var fs = require('fs');
2
3    function home() {
4      return fs.readFileSync('views/home.html');
5    }
```

So that the programming won't become excessively complex, it would be best to pass on the requirements in asynchronously working logic. Thus *response* object is handed over and the call of "write" and "end" now takes place over there.

File: start.js

```
1    var http = require("http");
2    var url = require("url");
3
4    function start(route, handler) {
5      function onRequest(request, response) {
6        var pathname = url.parse(request.url).pathname;
7        var content = route(pathname, handler, response);
8        if (!content) {
9          response.writeHead(404, {
10            "Content-Type": "text/plain"
11          });
12          response.write("404 Not found");
13          response.end();
14        }
15      }
16      var port = process.env.port || 1337;
17      http.createServer(onRequest).listen(port);
18      console.log("Server started.");
19    }
20
21    exports.start = start;
```

The actual output was passed on to the logic (line 7). Only the case of an error is still treated here.

The logic begins with the abstraction over the router, which can be steered by the inversely connected configuration from the outside. The return of the output takes place with the call of the function in line 4 of the file *router.js*.

File: router.js

```
1    function route(pathname, handler, response) {
2      console.log("Request for " + pathname);
3      if (typeof handler[pathname] === 'function') {
4        return handler[pathname](response);
5      } else {
6        console.log("No Method found for " + pathname);
7        return null;
8      }
9    }
10   exports.route = route;
```

In the file *handlers.js,* the call is now made asynchronously and the answer is provided via callback function. The module "fs" (File System) is doing good work by sending these to the browser.

Cutout of handlers.js (asynchronously)

```
1   var fs = require('fs');
2
3   function home(response) {
4     fs.readFile('views/home.html', function (err, data) {
5       response.writeHead(200, {
6         "Content-Type": "text/html"
7       });
8       response.write(data);
9       response.end();
10    });
11    return true;
12  }
```

Dynamic HTML

Without Template System, much HTML must be provided manually. Sometimes it is enough, but the following example also shows why Template Engines such as Pug are so famous.

The following extension assumes a folder with the name *files* exists. The function *shows* of the business logic is used in order to show all files in this folder.

Cutout of handlers.js (asynchronously)

```
1   var fs = require('fs');
2
3   function show(response) {
4     fs.readdir('files', function (err, list) {
5       response.writeHead(200, { "Content-Type": "text/html" });
6       var html = '<html><head></head>' +
7                  '<body><h1>File Manager</h1>';
8       if (list.length) {
9         html += "<ul>";
10        for (i = 0; i < list.length; i++) {
11          html += '<li><a href="/show?fn=' +
12                  list[i] + '">' +
13                  list[i] + '</a></li>';
14        }
15        html += "</ul>";
16      } else {
17        html += '<h2>No files found</h2>';
18      }
19      html += '</body></html>';
20      response.write(html);
21      response.end();
22    });
23    return true;
24  }
```

Here the folder with 'fs.readdir' is read and a list of hyperlinks is created, one for each file. Now the files must arrive in the folder.

Sending HTML Files

First change the HTML file which is to be sent to the browser, as shown subsequently.

File: views/home.html

```
1   <html>
2     <head>
3       <meta http-equiv="Content-Type"
4               content="text/html; charset=UTF-8" />
5     </head>
6     <body>
7       <h1>File Manager</h1>
8       <a href="/show">Show all Files</a>
9
10      <form action="/upload" method="post">
11      <input type="file" />
12      <input type="submit" value="Upload file" />
13      </form>
14    </body>
15  </html>
```

Now the logic already is able to load an HTML page from the hard disk and send it to the browser. In addition, it can show all files.

As coding (encoding), UTF-8 was selected here.

ⓘ UTF-8 Nowadays, all browsers support UTF-8 and the coding of special characters and umlauts are thereby absolutely possible. The "old" HTML entities such as & uum; for "ü" are obsolete. HTML 5 permits the information to the coding in minutes over the head field *Content-Type* or in the HTML head on one of the following Meta tags:

`<meta charset="utf-8" /> <meta http-equiv="Content-Type" ' content="text/html; charset=utf-8" />'`

The information is to that extent somewhat irritating, since the character set (charset) is originally Unicode and this character set is then coded by the means of UTF-8. As developer you must only know that you send HTML pages as UTF-8 and then the suitable head field.

In the last example, the function *upload* is missing for the completion. Transferring files takes place together with other form data with the help of HTTP verb POST. Sending settles the browser if a form is used. The next step consists first of recognizing and limiting the verbs.

Restriction of Verbs

The already shown Code functions, however Node reacts to all HTTP verbs. That is critical in practice, because unreasonable ways are opened into the application. The restriction thus consists of reacting only to GET and/or POST.

POST is only needed, in order to transport data from the browser to the server. The server thus receives all other requests only with GET.

File: handlers.js

```
1    var fs = require('fs');
2
3    function home(request, response) {
4      if (request.method !== 'GET') {
5        response.writeHead("405");
6        response.end();
7      }
8      fs.readFile('views/home.html', function (err, data) {
9        response.writeHead(200, { "Content-Type": "text/html" });
10       response.write(data);
11       response.end();
12     });
13     return true;
14   }
15   function show(request, response) {
16     if (request.method !== 'GET') {
17       response.writeHead("405");
18       response.end();
19     }
20     fs.readdir('files', function (err, list) {
21       response.writeHead(200, { "Content-Type": "text/html" });
22       var html = '<html><head></head>' +
23                     '<body><h1>File Manager</h1>';
24       if (list.length) {
25         html += "<ul>";
26         for (i = 0; i < list.length; i++) {
27           html += '<li><a href="/show?fn=' + list[i] + '">' + list[i] \
28   +
29                       '</a></li>';
30         }
31         html += "</ul>";
32       } else {
33         html += '<h2>No files found</h2>';
34       }
35       html += '</body></html>';
36       response.write(html);
37       response.end();
38     });
39     return true;
40   }
41   function upload(request, response) {
42       if (request.method !== 'POST') {
```

```
43          response.writeHead("405");
44          response.end();
45      }
46      return true;
47  }
48  exports.home = home;
49  exports.show = show;
50  exports.upload = upload;
```

Since the requested verb stands in the requirement *request*, this parameter must also be handed over. In the file *start.js* line 7 now looks as follows:

```
var content = route(pathname, handler, request, response);
```

In the file *router.js* this now looks as follows:

File: router.js

```
1   function route(pathname, handler, request, response) {
2       console.log("Anforderung für " + pathname);
3       if (typeof handler[pathname] === 'function') {
4           return handler[pathname](request, response);
5       } else {
6           console.log("No method found " + pathname);
7           return null;
8       }
9   }
10  exports.route = route;
```

Handling Form Data

On the lowest level, the form data are passed on as simple byte sequence. Since still no helpful libraries are in use here, the processing must take place. It is up to the server to prepare the data. Before the method *upload* is called, the data should already be present.

The "request" object makes some events available in order to be able to react to data. The delivery of *request* already takes place in the preceding step, so that only few changes are necessary. The events "data" are usable here, when the data arrives, and "end" if no more data is present.

```
1   request.addListener("data", function(chunk) {
2       // Daten empfangen
3   });
4   request.addListener("end", function() {
5       // Keine Daten mehr
6   });
```

The event "data" is called several times. You must collect the data and then completely hand it over to the appropriate method. To *handlers.js* the parameter *postData* is introduced, so that—if available—the data is to be handed over. Now only the file *start.js* must be extended, thus the data can be evaluated, and *router.js* is used to pass on functions.

File: start.js

```
1    var http = require("http");
2    var url = require("url");
3
4    function start(route, handler) {
5      function onRequest(request, response) {
6        var pathname = url.parse(request.url).pathname;
7        var content;
8        var postData = '';
9        request.setEncoding("utf8");
10       if (request.method === 'POST') {
11         request.addListener("data", function (chunk) {
12           postData += chunk;
13         });
14         request.addListener("end", function () {
15           content = route(handler, pathname,
16                             request, response, postData);
17         });
18       } else {
19         content = route(handler, pathname, response);
20       }
21       var content = route(pathname, handler,
22                           request, response);
23
24       if (!content) {
25         response.writeHead(404, {
26           "Content-Type": "text/plain"
27         });
28         response.write("404 Not found");
29         response.end();
30       }
31     }
32     var port = process.env.port || 1337;
33     http.createServer(onRequest).listen(port);
34     console.log("Server gestartet.");
35   }
36
37   exports.start = start;
```

In line 5 a variable is defined, which takes up the form data. Starting from line 12 the two event working methods follow, in which the data is collected. If no more data follows, then the call of the router and thus the call of the suitable method takes place in line 16. If no data is present (for example with GET), then the router method is called directly.

File: router.js

```
1    function route(pathname, handler,
2                   request, response, postData) {
3      console.log("Request for " + pathname);
4      if (typeof handler[pathname] === 'function') {
5        return handler[pathname](request, response, postData);
```

```
 6    } else {
 7      console.log("No method found for " + pathname);
 8      return null;
 9    }
10  }
11  exports.route = route;
```

The value in *postData* is simply handed through. If it is "zero" or "undefined," then this JavaScript is also passed on. An error handling is not necessary here.

Processing Form Data

Form data is processed in HTTP in different ways. The simplest case is simple form fields. Then the data is located in form of a chain of parts of keys in the requirement:

```
Name=Joerg+Krause&Age=52&Formula=a+%2B+b+%3D%3D+13%25%21
```

However, if files are uploaded, these are often binary and must be coded accordingly. The receiver must now know how to provide the original binary format from the coded data. In addition, there is the MIME standard (Multipurpose Internet Mail Extensions). Originally this was developed in order to embed pictures in e-mails.

 POST and MIME   A very comprehensive representation about POST can be found on Wikipedia [2].

Likewise, a lot of information is to be found about MIME[3]. The examples from this section originate from these Wikipedia articles.

With Mime the coding of a file then looks as follows:

```
 1  MIME-Version: 1.0
 2  Content-Type: multipart/mixed; boundary=frontier
 3
 4  This is a message with multiple parts in MIME format.
 5  --frontier
 6  Content-Type: text/plain
 7
 8  This is the body of the message.
 9  --frontier
10  Content-Type: application/octet-stream
11  Content-Transfer-Encoding: base64
12
13  PGhObWw+CiAgPGhlYWQ+CiAgPC9oZWFkPgogIDxib2R5PgogICAgPHA+VGhpcyBpcyB0\
14  aGUg
15  Ym9keSBvZiB0aGUgbWVzc2FnZS48L3A+CiAgPC9ib2R5Pgo8L2h0bWw+Cg==
16  --frontier--
```

---

[2]https://en.wikipedia.org/wiki/POST_(HTTP)
[3]https://en.wikipedia.org/wiki/MIME#Form-Data

Both representations suggest that the processing of form data is not trivial, particularly since the examples show only a small part of the possibilities. It is at this time necessary to go back to further **npm** library stuff. A good start is the library *formidable*.

Install *formidable* first. Make it optionally also available globally (Option '-g'), in order to use it in other projects:

```
npm install formidable@latest --save -g
```

A file arriving via POST can be received thereby as follows:

```
1   var formidable = require('formidable'),
2       http = require('http'),
3       util = require('util');
4
5   http.createServer(function(req, res) {
6     if (req.url == '/upload' && req.method === 'POST') {
7       // Parser
8       var form = new formidable.IncomingForm();
9
10      form.parse(req, function(err, fields, files) {
11        res.writeHead(200, {'content-type': 'text/plain'});
12        res.write('Dateien: ');
13        res.end(files.length);
14      });
15
16      return;
17    }
18
19    // Formular
20    res.writeHead(200, {'content-type': 'text/html'});
21    res.end(
22      '<form action="/upload" enctype="multipart/form-data" ' +
23          'method="post">'+
24      '<input type="text" name="title"><br>'+
25      '<input type="file" name="upload" multiple="multiple">'+
26      '<br /><input type="submit" value="Upload">'+
27      '</form>'
28    );
29  }).listen(8080);
```

The organization of the form is important here. In line 19 is "enctype=multipart/form-data". With this attribute, coding is caused after MIME. Now another input element is needed that the file on the hard disk of the user selects (line 21). The method "parse" will then examine the files and make them available (line 10).

Q **Documentation**   The module *formidable* can be found on Github[4].

---

[4]https://github.com/felixge/node-formidable

The processing method *parse* returns two objects, *files* and *fields*. In it, the files and other fields of the form are to be found. The structure looks as follows:

```
1   fields: { title: 'Hello World' }
2
3   files: {
4     upload: {
5       size: 1558,
6       path: '/tmp/1c747974a27a6292743669e91f29350b',
7       name: 'us-flag.png',
8       type: 'image/png',
9       lastModifiedDate: Tue, 21 Jun 2011 07:02:41 GMT,
10      _writeStream: [Object],
11      length: [Getter],
12      filename: [Getter],
13      mime: [Getter]
14      }
15    }
16  }
```

The information *path* is interesting. This is the temporary place where the files were, for a start, put down. From there it can now—if all other basic conditions fit—be copied into the application folder.

Handling Querystring

The indicator method should serve to offer the files for downloading. In addition, a parameter is handed over: the file name. The delivery of data into HTTP by the means of URL is made by the part after the question mark, the Querystring. Also for the processing of the data there's a specific module in Node:

```
var querystring = require("querystring")
```

A separate installation of the module is not necessary. Because of its outstanding importance, it is always available. In the application, the links are then produced dynamically for the files and embedded in the existing HTML. The file names hang as parameters on the links in the form of *fn=filename*. The Querystring must be examined thus for the field *fn*.

The call of the data then looks as follows:

```
querystring.parse(request.url.querystring).fn
```

The result is the file name or "undefined," if the parameter was not found. The finished *show* function now looks as follows:

File: handlers.js

```
1   var fs = require("fs");
2
3   function home(response, postData) {
4     // Unchanged
5   }
```

```
6    function show(response, postData) {
7      if (response.Method !== 'GET') {
8        response.write("405 Method not allowed");
9      }
10     console.log("Request 'show' called.");
11
12     response.write();
13     response.end();
14   }
15   function upload(response, postData) {
16     // unchanged
17   }
18   exports.home = home;
19   exports.show = show;
20   exports.upload = upload;
```

The Querystring is in *request*. This object is already passed on. However, it is meaningful to dissolve the distinction between data from GET and from POST and work only with data. That can take place in the previous layer outside of the logic, so that all methods of the business logic profit from it. The two verbs are mutually exclusive; conflicts will therefore never occur. The server thereby supplies either the data over "form.parse" or over "querystring.parse". In both cases it concerns a JavaScript object.

The complete Application

With this code the application can be finished. The components are:

- an HTML page, which serves as home page and for the announcement of all files. On this page is also the form for uploads

- the server, which receives requirements, prepares and hands them over to the router

- the router, which recognizes the paths:

    – */home* back to the homepage

    – */show* for downloading a file

    – */upload* for uploading a file

- a small business logic, which processes and makes the data available

Practically each Web application is similarly developed, although much more complex. The primitive internal structure of Node leads the direct access to enormous performance and is nearly boundless. However, you are well advised as developer, with the bases of protocols and elementary techniques, to argue with computer science (HTTP, MIME, coding with UTF-8, etc.).

Here the finished program, consisting of:

- *server.js*

- *start.js*

- *router.js*

- *handler.js*

- *home.html*

On the main system the folder *files* must still be configured, so that the process under which Node is implemented can (and only there) have rights for writing, so that uploading the files functions.

The finished program still uses another Node library: *mime*. It serves the determination of the correct *content-type* head fields when downloading the files. Install it as follows:

```
npm install mime --save
```

The Application *server.js*

The application starts in the file *server.js*. Here the other modules are merged. In relation to the previous versions, the agreement of the routes is not only because of the names but also because of the suitable HTTP verb bind. Thus the individual, repetitive inquiry of the method is no longer necessary.

File: server.js

```
1    var server = require("./start");
2    var router = require("./router");
3    var requestHandlers = require("./handlers");
4
5    var handler = {};
6    handler[["/", 'GET']] = requestHandlers.home;
7    handler[["/show", 'GET']] = requestHandlers.show;
8    handler[["/upload", 'POST']] = requestHandlers.upload;
9
10   server.start(router.route, handler);
```

The Starting Script *start.js*

The function start itself is accordingly extended. On the one hand, the method of execution is shifted into the new function *execute*, since it is needed several times. The business logic worries again about sending the data. Only if this fails, the generic error *400 Bad Request* is sent.

⚠ **Bad Request**   Often one thinks too long and hard about which HTTP code is suitable for announcing errors to the client. That is not worth the trouble. The user can begin in the long run with no message and see meaning in it. It will always be discussed with a general error page. Concrete errors are rather dangerous, because if rather than a regular user attacks the server, each error message referring to further attack potential multiplies. The generic error *400 Bad Request* does not state anything, except that the action failed.

In the script some modules are used. *http, url* and *querystring* are internally available in Node. *formidable* has been additionally installed via **npm**. In the method *onRequest*, the path for Routing is determined and the Querystring is extracted (line 16). At POST, the evaluating of the form data takes place.

ℹ **POST and Querystring**   Theoretically, a POST requirement can also have data in the Querystring. Such mixtures may not be a good idea, but the general inquiry of Querystring data is correct.

From the data the *data* object will be created, so that form data, Querystring data, and uploaded files can be handed over to the business logic.

File: start.js

```
1   var http = require("http");
2   var url = require("url");
3   var formidable = require("formidable");
4   var querystring = require("querystring");
5
6   function start(route, handler) {
7
8     function execute(pathname, handler, request, response, data) {
9       var content = route(pathname, handler,
10                             request, response, data);
11      if (!content) {
12        response.writeHead(400, {
13          "Content-Type": "text/plain"
14        });
15        response.write("400 Bad request");
16        response.end();
17      }
18    }
19
20    function onRequest(request, response) {
21      var pathname = url.parse(request.url).pathname;
22      var query = url.parse(request.url).query;
23      if (request.method === 'POST') {
24        var form = new formidable.IncomingForm();
25        form.parse(request, function (err, fields, files) {
26          if (err) {
27            console.error(err.message);
28            return;
29          }
30          var data = { fields: fields, files: files };
31          execute(pathname, handler, request, response, data);
32        });
33      }
34      if (request.method === 'GET') {
35        var data = {
36          fields: querystring.parse(query)
37        };
38        execute(pathname, handler, request, response, data);
39      }
40    }
41    var port = process.env.port || 1337;
42    http.createServer(onRequest).listen(port);
43    console.log("Server gestartet.");
44  }
45
46  exports.start = start;
```

Nothing changed on the server itself. This part corresponds to the previous examples.

The Routing Functions *router.js*

The router is unchanged to a large extent. The only adjustment concerns the use of the path and HTTP verb with the choice of the required method in case of any array: "[pathname, method]". Only the answer *response* is handed over, because the implementing methods should send their data themselves, and the determined data of the requirement. So the requirement does not have to be passed on any longer.

File: router.js

```
1   function route(pathname, handler, request, response, data) {
2     console.log("Request for " + pathname);
3     var method = request.method;
4     if (typeof handler[[pathname, method]] === 'function') {
5       return handler[[pathname, method]](response, data);
6     } else {
7       console.log("No action found for " + pathname +
8                   " and method " + method);
9       return null;
10    }
11  }
12  exports.route = route;
```

The Business Logic *handler.js*

The business logic covers the three methods, which "do something":

- *home*: call of the home page with the form for uploading

- *show*: display of all uploaded files or downloading of a file

- *upload*: uploading a file and transferring it to *show*

File: handler.js (home)

```
1   var fs = require('fs');
2   var path = require('path');
3   var mime = require('mime');
4
5   function home(response, data) {
6     fs.readFile('views/home.html', function (err, data) {
7       response.writeHead(200, { "Content-Type": "text/html" });
8       response.write(data);
9       response.end();
10    });
11    return true;
12  }
```

Here the HTML file is asynchronously read and then supplied to the client.

There are two actions in show. First, the parameter 'fn' is checked. If there is a filename within, the file will be read synchronously and delivered for download. If there is no such parameter, an HTML page will be created dynamically, that shows all files in the folder as hyperlinks. The download will be controlled by special header fields that you can create using response.setHeader.

Now sending the files uses response.end. That's a conjunction of write and end. The setting 'binary' is mandatory, otherwise Node would try to treat the content as plain text and encode the content as UTF-8. That would destroy any binary content, such as images.

Datei: handler.js (show)

```
1   function show(response, data) {
2     // Herunterladen
3     if (data.fields && data.fields['fn']) {
4       var name = data.fields['fn'];
5       var file = path.join(__dirname, '/files', name);
6       var mimeType = mime.lookup(file);
7       response.setHeader('Content-disposition',
8                          'attachment; filename=' + name);
9       response.setHeader('Content-type', mimeType);
10      var filedata = fs.readFileSync(file, 'binary');
11      response.end(filedata, 'binary');
12      return true;
13    }
14    // Show all
15    fs.readdir('files', function (err, list) {
16      response.writeHead(200, { "Content-Type": "text/html" });
17      var html = '<html><head></head>' +
18                 '<body><h1>File Manager</h1>';
19      if (list.length) {
20        html += "<ul>";
21        for (i = 0; i < list.length; i++) {
22          html += '<li><a href="/show?fn=' + list[i] + '">' +
23                  list[i] + '</a></li>';
24        }
25        html += "</ul>";
26      } else {
27        html += '<h2>No files found</h2>';
28      }
29      html += '</body></html>';
30      response.write(html);
31      response.end();
32    });
33    return true;
34  }
```

The third part is the function for uploading. Even that is based on parameters, particularly the field "fn" from the HTML form. The copy function is using *copyFile*, which uses Streams and is particularly efficient. The function is programmed asynchronously and informs the callers about the callback function *callback*, if the action is final. The function *upload* continues to lead to the summary page *show*, so that the user can inform himself about the success of the action.

File: handler.js (upload)

```
1   function upload(response, data) {
2     // Upload
3     var temp = data.files['fn'].path;
```

```
4     var name = data.files['fn'].name;
5     copyFile(temp, path.join('./files', name), function (err) {
6       if (err) {
7         console.log(err);
8         return false;
9       } else {
10        // Dateiliste anzeigen
11        return show(response, data);
12      }
13    });
14    return true;
15  }
16
17  function copyFile(source, target, callback) {
18      var rd = fs.createReadStream(source);
19      rd.on('error', function (err) { callback(err); });
20      var wr = fs.createWriteStream(target);
21      wr.on('error', function (err) { callback(err); });
22      wr.on('finish', function () { callback(); });
23      rd.pipe(wr);
24  }
25
26  exports.home = home;
27  exports.show = show;
28  exports.upload = upload;
```

The data in "data.files[fn]" offers far more than only name and path. So information can be made here about the type of file, the file size and the date.

ⓘ **Server versus Client Upload**   The version presented here uses so-called server uploading. The client may send everything. The server stores the data in a temporary listing and then makes it available. The server script then decides what happens with the data. That has the disadvantage that the user possibly transfers large or inadmissible files, he experiences a long waiting time, and then gets an error message. Client page upload functions can be programmed in JavaScript in the browser and then transfer only if it is meaningful and promising. This is not dealt with here.

Template of the HTML Page *home.html*

As the latter, the form page shall be presented again. This serves to branch out to the page with the list of the files and it contains the form for uploading.

File: home.html

```
1   <html>
2   <head>
3     <meta http-equiv="Content-Type"
4           content="text/html; charset=UTF-8" />
5   </head>
```

```
6    <body>
7      <h1>Dateimanager</h1>
8      <a href="/show">Zeige alle Dateien</a>
9      <hr />
10     <form action="/upload" method="post"
11           enctype="multipart/form-data">
12       <input type="file" name="fn" />
13       <input type="submit" value="Upload file" />
14     </form>
15   </body>
16   </html>
```

Pay attention to the names of the input element "file" name="fn".

This name must agree with the value used in the code "fn". Important is also the following attribute:

```
enctype="multipart/form-data"
```

This permits the coding of the files for the transmission with HTTP. If you would like to process only form data, but no files, then you omit the attribute.

Summary

This chapter showed a first, compact introduction to Node. As far as possible, no additional libraries were inserted such as *Express* or Template Engines such as *Pug*. Refer to the further chapters to read more about Express and Pug and how they simplify your life as a developer. Since Node is quite simple, some actions, which are due to protocol HTTP, had to be programmed. But there are naturally many finished solutions. The next chapter will concentrate on overviews, documentation and the most important modules of Node which will be presented, with which first applications can be developed.

CHAPTER 4

The Most Important Node Modules

This chapter shows the most important modules, with which elementary tasks in a Web application can be settled. Thereby it concerns the actual Node library.

Global Modules

Gobal modules are always present and do not have to be agreed upon.

Timer

Interval timers abstract to a large extent the possibilities offered according to standard by JavaScript. Absolutely use the Node variant, in order to get no problems later with other parallel running modules.

setTimeout

This instruction agrees upon the call of the callback function after a certain period in milliseconds. Optionally, arguments can be indicated. The function gives an object of the type "timeoutObject", which can be used with "clearTimeout()".

Syntax: setTimeout(callback, delay[, arg][, ...])

⚠ **Real Time**   Node is not real time–capable and does not guarantee that the call of time-controlled callback function takes place accurately at the agreed-upon function.

---

clearTimeout

This function prevents the call.

Syntax: clearTimeout(timeoutObject)

© Jörg Krause 2017
J. Krause, *Programming Web Applications with Node, Express and Pug*, DOI 10.1007/978-1-4842-2511-0_4

setInterval

This function also corresponds to the internal JavaScript function; however, it runs under the control of Node. The callback function is called repetitive at expiration of the interval. The function gives an object of the type `intervalObject`, which can be used with `clearInterval()`.

Syntax: `setInterval(callback, delay[, arg][, ...])`

clearInterval

This function stops the repetitive call.

Syntax: `clearInterval(intervalObject)`

unref

This method is offered by the objects `timeoutObject` and `intervalObject`. If a Node application ends, and interval timers are still in action, the execution is continued nevertheless, until the last interval timer ran off. With `unref`, it can be shown that the completion of the application stops and does not continue to implement the remaining interval timers. The repeated call of `unref` on the same object does not have an effect.

The functions shift the interval timer into the major loop of the application. Too many such interval timers can affect the achievement of the major loop. They should `unref` from there consciously and only if absolutely necessary.

ref

Before with `unref` into the major loop transferred interval timer can go back to its regular condition with this function. The repeated call does not have an effect.

setImmediate / clearImmediate

The method `setImmediate` is a more highly priotizied interval timer, which releases after I/O events and is called before `setTimeout` and `setInterval`. This interval timer gives an object `immediateObject` back, which can be used with `clearImmediate()`. Several callback functions are placed in a queue and processed in order, as they were defined. The execution of the queue takes place once per run of the major loop of the application. A new placed object is thus then implemented only if the major loop goes through next time.

Syntax: `setImmediate(callback[, arg][, ...])`

`clearImmediate` stops the execution of the timer indicated by `immediateObject`.

Syntax: `clearImmediate(immediateObject)`

Global Objects

Global objects are active in all modules. They do not have to be agreed upon separately.

global

This is the global name area. A variable in JavaScript is global in the global name area, even if it was defined with var. In Node this is not the case—the global name area is always the current module. Only by explicit access to global does a global name area become possible.

process

The process object shows information about the process.

console

With this object you have access to the console.

Buffer

The buffer obect contains the handling of buffered data.

require

This function requests a module. This function is not really global, but in each module it is automatically agreed upon locally, so that it is always available like a global function.

The method require.resolve uses the search mechanism for modules, but doesn't load the module in case of success, but instead returns the path under which it was found. Modules can be locally or globally installed, so that the discovery page quite varies. With require.cache, modules within the object are cached if they return the features. If the module is removed from the cache by deletion of the key, the next call of 'require' will load the module again.

__filename

This is the file name of the up-to-date implemented code file. The name contains the dissolved, absolute path. This does not have to be the same path that the command line tool used. If the call takes place in a module, the module is the implemented code file and the path points to the module.

If, for example, the file *example.js* is implemented in the path */User/joerg/Apps*, the following call */User/joerg/Apps/example.js* returns:

```
console.log(__filename);
```

__filename is globally usable, however, in each module in which it is locally defined.

__dirname

This is the listing in which the up-to-date implemented file is. If, for example, the file *example.js* is implemented in the path /User/joerg/Apps*, the following call */User/joerg/Apps* returns:

```
console.log(__dirname);
```

__dirname is globally usable; however, in each module it is locally defined.

module

This is a reference to the current module. The feature `module.exports` is used to make the functions exported by the module available. They are made available by the call of `require()`.

    `module` is globally usable; however, in each module it is locally defined.

exports

This is an alias for `module.exports` and shortens only the writing effort.

    `exports` is globally usable; however, it is locally defined in each module.

HTTP and HTTPS

With the HTTP and HTTPS modules, almost all HTTP and HTTPS modules are supported. Communication on this level is very elementary. Frameworks such as *Express* abstract this and rely on *http*. Nevertheless, it can be meaningful for many cases to implement protocol actions directly.

    Node can deal with Streams—thus there is a sequential river of bytes. This is way more effective than holding the entire data for one procedure in only one memory (buffering). The *http* module worries about processing data with Streams and faciliates programming substantially.

Basics

HTTP consists of a command line and head fields, which describe the instruction more clearly. In Node, the head fields are made available as JSON. An appropriate object would thus look as follows:

```
1  {
2    'content-length': '123',
3    'content-type': 'text/plain',
4    'connection': 'keep-alive',
5    'host': 'mysite.com',
6    'accept': '*/*'
7  }
```

The keys are always converted according to the specification in small letters. The values are never changed. That is already the whole interface of Node. Generally, Node is very simple with this module. Neither the head fields nor contents of a message are examined, evaluated, or treated internally.

    Head fields, which have several values use "," (comma) for the separation of the values. The only exceptions are the head fields for Cookies, which an array accepts. If fields permit only one value, Node controls this and throws an exception.

    Arriving or sent head fields are made available as a rough object. This is an array with sequential pairs of keys and values that looks as follows:

```
1  [ 'Content-Length', '123456',
2    'content-type', 'text/plain',
3    'CONNECTION', 'keep-alive',
4    'Host', 'mysite.com',
5    'accept', '*/*' ]
```

Transformation and control actions take place thereafter so that the head files actually made available or sent can deviate from it.

Fields

The section describes fields, which make values available and which refer to the internal configuration.

http.METHODS returns in the form of arrays a list with HTTP verbs, which are supported. http.STATUS_codes is an array with the status codes, which know HTTP and the assigned summary. For 404 this is defined exemplarily as follows:

```
http.STATUS_CODES[404] === 'Not Found'
```

Methods

The methods make the appropriate actions possible regarding the protocol processing "http.createServer" a new instance of the HTTP server returns. Thus HTTP requests can be received and processed. The syntax looks as follows:

```
http.createServer([requestListener])
```

The callback function *requestListener* is a method, which gets the received data.

With http.request(option[,callback]), Node sends a request to another server. Node is thus, in this case, the client. Node uses several connections, if this is possible. However, the method treats this internally, so that you must give no consideration with programming to it. The following syntax is used:

```
http.request(options [, callback])
```

The options can be JSON or a character string. If it is a character string, url.parse() will automatically be used, in order to parse the character string. The callback method supplies an object with the answer (response).

The options have the following meaning:

- *host*: the domain name or the IP address, where the request is sent. Without information, this is called "localhost."

- *hostname*: If url.parse() is used, you should use *hostname* instead of *host*.

- *port*: the port for the request. Standard is the port 80.

- *localAddress*: If you have several network cards, you can hereby instruct which local address (network card with the appropriate connection) is to be used by Node.

- *socketPath*: Under Unix, this refers to Unix domain Sockets.

- These are terminals for interprocess communication. You can use this on a local system or host:port syntax.

- *method*: The verb (HTTP method) is in capital letters. Default value is here: GET.

- *path*: the path to resources for the requirement. The default value is '/'. The path should contain the Querystring, if this is to be used, e.g., */index.html?=12*. Illegal indications lead to an exception.

- *headers*: a JSON object with the information of the header fields

- *auth*: the kind of authentication. It produces the header field.

- *Authorization*.

- *agent*: the behavior of the Clients steers. If the information takes place, the head field *Connection: keep-alive* is produced. Possible values for this parameter are:

  - undefined (default): Global information for the mentioned combination is *host* and *port*.

  - object of the type agent: explicit information of all values

  - No connecting pool is formed. Each request ends with *Connection: close*.

- *keepAlive*: The connection is kept open in a connecting pool, so that other connecting desires can access at a later time. The standard is `false`.

- *keepAliveMsecs*: If *keepAlive* is used, hereby the time can be indicated in milliseconds, to which a TCP package is sent as a sign of life. The default value is 1000.

The method gives an instant to the class `http.ClientRequest` back. This is a writable stream. For the request, if data is needed (for example because during a POST requirement a form is sent), then these data will be written in the stream.

```
1   var postData = querystring.stringify({
2     'msg' : 'Hello World!'
3   });
4
5   var options = {
6     hostname: 'www.google.com',
7     port: 80,
8     path: '/upload',
9     method: 'POST',
10    headers: {
11      'Content-Type': 'application/x-www-form-urlencoded',
12      'Content-Length': postData.length
13    }
14  };
15
16  var req = http.request(options, function(res) {
17    console.log('STATUS: ' + res.statusCode);
18    console.log('HEADERS: ' + JSON.stringify(res.headers));
19    res.setEncoding('utf8');
20    res.on('data', function (chunk) {
21      console.log('BODY: ' + chunk);
22    });
23  });
24
25  req.on('error', function(e) {
26    console.log('problem with request: ' + e.message);
27  });
28
29  req.write(postData);
30  req.end();
```

The actual writing takes place with `req.write(postData)`. The use of `req.end()` is necessary here because the stream is otherwise closed. After terminating, no further data can be written. The requirement object *req* knows an even `error`, to which you can react in order to intercept errors. Errors can occur if one of the procedures fails with sending (dissolution of DNS, TCP error, error when parsing the head fields, etc.).

If the head filed *Connection: keep-alive* is manually inserted, Node recognizes this and keeps the connection open until the next request is sent.

If the head field *Content-length* is sent, then the use of computer field is switched off. Computer field is block-by-block sending of data. The information takes place via the head field *Transfer- Encoding: chunked*.

If an *Except* head field is used, then the head fields are sent immediately. After *Expect: 100-continue*, you should listen immediately to the appropriate event (with timeout). RFC2616 section 8.2.3 gives more information in addition.

If the head field *Authorization* is indicated, the data produced by the option auth is overwritten.

With http.get a shortened variant of the method request stands ready, the one request initiated by means of GET. Since no data is sent with GET, req.end() produces it automatically:

```
http.get(options[, callback])
```

An example shows how it goes:

```
1  http.get("http://www.google.com/index.html", function(res) {
2    console.log("Got response: " + res.statusCode);
3  }).on('error', function(e) {
4    console.log("Got error: " + e.message);
5  });
```

Classes

Some classes supply further functionality.

http.Server

The HTTP server offers an environment which reacts to actions of protocols by means of events. The events are:

- **request:** function (request, response) { }

  Each arriving request releases this event. If the connection remains open (*Keep Alive*), then it can be that several events per request are released. The parameter *request* of the type http.IncomingMessage and *response* is "http.ServerResponse".

- **connection:** function (socket) { }

  Releases, if the TCP stream object was opened. The parameter *socket* is of the type net.Socket.

- **close:** function () { }

  Releases, if the connection was closed.

- **checkContinue:** function (request, response) { }

  This event reacts to *Expect: 100-continue*. If that is not treated, the server reacts automatically with *100 Continue*. If a treatment takes place, then it must be reacted with response.writeContinue(), if data is to be sent. Otherwise, communication with *400 Bad Request* or a comparable error will happen. If this event is produced and treated, request won't be released.

- **connect:** function (request, socket, head) { }

  Releases, if the client is connected by means of HTTP CONNECT. The parameter *request* is http.IncomingMessage. The parameter *socket* is of the type net.Socket. *head* against it is an instance of buffer.

- **upgrade:** function (request, socket, head) { }

  With opened connection, this event is released if a client wants to upgrade the connection. The parameter *request* is of the type http.IncomingMessage. The parameter *socket* is of the type "net.Socket". *head*, however, is an instance of buffer. An upgrade is in principle a protocol change, e.g., from HTTP 1.1. to HTTP 2.0. to WebSockets, to IRC, etc. In practice, this is relevant only for WebSockets. In addition, look at the following information: Draft[1].

- **clientError:** function (exception, socket) { }

  If the client supplies an eror, this event will be treated.

  The parameter *socket* is of the type net.Socket.

The events are reached by means of the method on:

```
1  var http = require("http");
2  var server = http.createServer();
3
4  server.on("request", function (req, res) {
5      res.end("this is the response");
6  });
7
8  server.listen(3000);
```

Methods for http.Server

The object *server* itself, the createServer, has some methods, which are likewise interesting.

With server.list, the server begins at the indicated port and the appropriate address—thus the Socket—to listen. If the host name is not indicated, all IP addresses on the machine are launched (only IPv4). The following variants exist:

```
server.listen(port[, hostname][, backlog][, callback]) server.listen(path[, callback])
server.listen(handle[, callback])
```

  On an Unix system, a Unix Socket in the form of a file names can be used instead of the host name.

Alternatively, the Socket path can be used. The other configuration parameters are then non-existing. On Windows, this is not supported:

---

[1]http://tools.ietf.org/html/draft-ietf-hybi-thewebsocketprotocol-17

The parameter *backlog* is the length of the buffer queue for arriving connections. If a connecting desire arrives and the procedure is still in processing, then Node takes up this request to this queue.

The default value is 511 (!sic). Values to 1,000 are meaningful. Long waiting times in Clients suggest that a connection is to be expected, while Node is also hardly able to process these.

If *handle* is used, then this is an object that describes the "server" or a "Socket."

The function is asynchronous and works with the callback method *callback*.

With server.close, the server stops accepting desired connections:

```
server.close([callback])
```

Since connections are not available, a value can be set with "server.setTimeout", which determines how long the waiting time will take:

```
server.setTimeout(msecs, callback)
```

The value is indicated in milliseconds. The default value amounts to two minutes. "server.timeout" shows the set value.

With server.maxHeadersCount, the number of head fields is limited. According to standard this is 1,000; with 0 the value is unlimited.

The class http.ServerResponse

An instance of this class is provided internally. This is the type, which is handed over by the parameter *response* in the callback function of the event "request." This is the answer object. It implements a writable stream. This works with events.

close: function () { }

shows that the connection was closed before end was able to send the data.
finish: function () { }

is released if the transmission of the answer is settled. For Node, this is the moment of the delivery to the operating system. It is not clear that the data leaves the compuer or that the client received it.

On an instance of this class, various operations are possible. response.writeContinue sends an *HTTP/1.1. 100 Continue* to the client to request that the data can be sent. With reponse.writeHead, Node sends the head (Status code plus head fields) to the client. The status code is the three-figure HTTP code, for example, 200 or 404. The head fields can be indicated accordingly. The following syntax is applicable:

```
response.writeHead(statusCode[, statusMessage][, headers])
1   var body = 'hello world';
2   response.writeHead(200, {
3     'Content-Length': body.length,
4     'Content-Type': 'text/plain' }
5   );
```

This method may be called only once and must happen before response.end().

Alternatively you can work with response.write() and response.end(). If response.write() is used and the answer hasn't been terminated yet, Node computes the head fields accumulated with the call of writeHead.

 Content Length The length head field contains the size in bytes. If the text is coded in UTF-8 or another procedure, that is not the number of indications. Use `Buffer.byteLength()` in order to determine the correct value. Node does not check whether the information fits in *Content-Length*.

With `response.setTimeout` the timeout value is set in milliseconds:

```
response.setTimeout(msecs, callback)
```

The callback function *callback* is called if the time runs out. If no information takes place upon completion, the appropriate objects for Socket, Server, Response, etc., are cleared up. However, if a callback function is present, then you must settle this in the function.

With `response.statusCode`, you specify which status code is used. This is not necessary if you work with `writeHead`.

```
response.statusCode = 404;
```

The feature contains the actual value after sending the answer.

Specify which status code is used with the `response.statusMessage` feature. This is not necessary if you work with `writeHead`. The information is only meaningful if you want to send something else as the standard text:

```
response.statusMessage = 'Not found';
```

The feature contains the actual value after sending the answer. `response.setHeader` produces a head field or replaces it, if it is already present in the list of head fields which can be sent. If several head fields are to be produced, you can use an array. The following syntax is valid:

```
response.setHeader(name, value)
```

```
1    response.setHeader("Content-Type", "text/html");
2    response.setHeader("Set-Cookie", ["type=ninja", "language=javascript\
3    "]);
```

Everyone can determine with `response.headersSent`, whether the head fields were already sent or not.

`response.sendDate` is a boolean feature that shows if the head field *Date* shall be produced. If this head field was already manually entered, the manual entry is not overwritten.

 In HTTP ist das Kopffeld *Date* ein Pflichtfeld. Sie sollten dies nur zu Testzwecken unterdrücken.

`response.getHeader` is a cunning head field, as long as it wasn't sent yet. After sending, no access is possible anymore. The name considers upper and lower case—all head field names are written in lower case internally. The syntax of this method is as follows:

```
response.getHeader(name)
```

```
1    var contentType = response.getHeader('content-type');
```

response.removeHeader removes a head field, as long as it was not sent yet:

```
1   response.removeHeader("Content-Encoding");
```

The method response.write writes a quantity of data. That leads to the fact that implicitly specified head fields are sent, because these will transfer before the data. If response.writeHead() was used before, the head fields defined there are used.

```
response.write(chunk[, encoding][, callback])
```

The method can be called several times, in order to transmit data block-by-block (chunks). The parameter *chunk* can be a character string or byte stream. If the data is a character string, the parameter determines *encoding*, and then how these are converted in bytes. The default value is "utf-8". The callback method *callback* is called, if the data was sent.

 The method serves for sending data on the lowest level. No processing of contents in any form takes place here.

The method returns true if the data was handed over to the internal buffer, false is returned if the data remained in the memory. "drain" is produced, if the buffer is empty again.

With response.addTrailers(headers), head fields are attached to the end of the message. That can be done only with data, which is supplied to the computer field.

```
1   response.writeHead(200, { 'Content-Type': 'text/plain',
2                              'Trailer': 'Content-MD5' });
3   response.write(fileData);
4   response.addTrailers({
5       'Content-MD5': "7895bf4b8828b55ceaf47747b4bca667"
6   });
7   response.end();
```

With "response.end" it is communicated that the transmission is terminated. This method **must** always be called.

```
response.end([data][, encoding][, callback])
```

If data is indicated internally, response.write(data, encoding) is called. The callback function is called if all data was sent.

Class http.ClientRequest

An instance of this class is provided through http.request(). This is the requirement object. The head fields are thereafter still alterable with the methods setHeader(name, value), getHeader(name), and removeHeader(name). Node is in this case the client, which sends requests to another server.

In order to get the answer of the produced and sent request, you hand an event treatment function over for the event response. The event returns an instance of the class IncomingMessage. If the answer should contain data, it can be accessed with the event data. Alternatively you can listen to it with the event readable and then read it actively with the event response.read().

Node does not check whether the information in *Content-Length* is correct and fits with the content. Do not rely on this value!

```
1   var http = require('http');
2   var net = require('net');
3   var url = require('url');
4
5   // Create proxy for tunnel
6   var proxy = http.createServer(function (req, res) {
7     res.writeHead(200, {'Content-Type': 'text/plain'});
8     res.end('okay');
9   });
10  proxy.on('connect', function(req, cltSocket, head) {
11    // Connect previous server
12    var srvUrl = url.parse('http://' + req.url);
13    var srvSocket = net.connect(srvUrl.port, srvUrl.hostname, 14
      function() {
15      cltSocket.write('HTTP/1.1 200 Connection Established\r\n' +
16                      'Proxy-agent: Node-Proxy\r\n' +
17                      '\r\n');
18      srvSocket.write(head);
19      srvSocket.pipe(cltSocket);
20      cltSocket.pipe(srvSocket);
21    }); // End function
22  });
23
24  // Proxy runs now
25  proxy.listen(1337, '127.0.0.1', function() {
26
27    // Anforderung erstellen
28    var options = {
29      port: 1337,
30      hostname: '127.0.0.1',
31      method: 'CONNECT',
32      path: 'www.google.com:80'
33    };
34
35    var req = http.request(options);
36    req.end();
37
38    req.on('connect', function(res, socket, head) {
39      console.log('got connected!');
40
41      // Anforderung über Tunnel
42      socket.write('GET / HTTP/1.1\r\n' +
43                   'Host: www.google.com:80\r\n' +
44                   'Connection: close\r\n' +
45                   '\r\n');
```

```
46        socket.on('data', function(chunk) {
47          console.log(chunk.toString());
48        });
49        socket.on('end', function() {
50          proxy.close();
51        });
52      });
53    });
```

A further event must be treated if necessary: upgrade. The callback function has the following signature:

```
function (response, socket, head)
```

An upgrade is necessary if the client liked to change the protocol, for example, from HTTP 1.1 to HTTP 2.0 or to WebSockets.

```
1    var http = require('http');
2
3    // Create an HTTP server
4    var srv = http.createServer(function (req, res) {
5      res.writeHead(200, {'Content-Type': 'text/plain'});
6      res.end('okay');
7    });
8    srv.on('upgrade', function(req, socket, head) {
9      socket.write('HTTP/1.1 101 Web Socket Protocol Handshake\r\n' +
10                   'Upgrade: WebSocket\r\n' +
11                   'Connection: Upgrade\r\n' +
12                   '\r\n');
13
14      socket.pipe(socket); // Echo zurück
15    });
16
17    // now that server is running
18    srv.listen(1337, '127.0.0.1', function() {
19
20      // make a request
21      var options = {
22        port: 1337,
23        hostname: '127.0.0.1',
24        headers: {
25          'Connection': 'Upgrade',
26          'Upgrade': 'websocket'
27        }
28      };
29
30      var req = http.request(options);
31      req.end();
32
33      req.on('upgrade', function(res, socket, upgradeHead) {
34        console.log('got upgraded!');
```

```
35        socket.end();
36        process.exit(0);
37    });
38  });
```

The event continue arises if the server sends a *100 Continue*, which usually is a reaction to the request *Expect: 100-continue*. This is the request for the client that the data of the message may be sent.

With request.flushHeaders(), a method is available which sends the head fields actively. Normally, Node buffers head fields and sends these not immediately if they are defined. Buffering serves the optimization, so that all head fields fit ideally into a TCP package. With flush() and flushHeaders(), the optimization mechanism is ignored.

The actual writing of the data is done by request.write(chunk[, encoding][, callback]) with block-by-block (chunk) sending of the data. The head field *['Transfer-Encoding', 'chunked']* should be used in order to show the receiving station that the blocks are used for this to work.

The argument *chunk* can be a buffer or a character string. The callback function is called if the data was sent.

With request.end([data][, encoding][, callback]), the requirement is terminated. If parts of the data were not sent yet, "flush" is forced. If blocks were used, now the final sequence "0\r\n\r\n" is sent.

With data the result is identical to the call of request.write(data, encoding), followed by request.end(callback). The callback function is called if the data was sent.

With request.abort(), the requirement can be canceled. With request.setTimeout(timeout[, callback]), the timeout value is specified.

http.IncomingMessage

An arriving message of the type IncomingMessage is produced by http.Server or http.ClientRequest. The object is handed over as the first argument request and/or response of the event. The object implements a readable stream, and some further methods and features, as well.

With the event close, it is shown that the connection was closed. This event can occur only once.

The feature message.httpVersion shows which HTTP version was used. That is, either "1.1" or "1.0", etc. To get access to the version details, response.httpVersionMajor and response.httpVersionMinor can be of help.

The head fields can be selected over message.headers. Head fields are always internally marked with small letters. The output means console.log(request.headers); and produces the following JSON object:

```
1  {
2    'user-agent': 'curl/7.22.0',
3    host: '127.0.0.1:8000',
4    accept: '*/*'
5  }
```

If you want to read the head fields directly, without the treatment of Node, message.rawHeaders would be the right choice. It is interesting here that this is no listing with pairs of keys, but an array with alternatively head fields and their values.

```
1  [
2    'user-agent',
3    'this is invalid because there can be only one',
4    'User-Agent',
5    'curl/7.22.0',
6    'Host',
```

```
7      '127.0.0.1:8000',
8      'ACCEPT',
9      '*/*'
10    ]
```

In the end event (and only there) the `message.trailers` and `message.rawTrailers` can be queried in blocks (chunks) and transferred. By means of Trailer, block-by-block the messages will correctly be put together.

A temporal delimitation of the processing of the message can be achieved with `message.setTimeout(msecs, callback)`. The information of the time effected is in milliseconds, after the expiration *callback* is called.

The used HTTP verb can be inferred from the feature `message.method`. In `message.url`, the URL stands for the requirement. These features function only if the object comes from `http.Server`. The following requirements should serve as examples:

```
1    GET /status?name=ryan HTTP/1.1\r\n
2    Accept: text/plain\r\n
3    \r\n
```

In `request.url` stands then: "/status?name=ryan" For processing, the URL serves parse:

```
1    var url = require('url');
2    console.log(url.parse('/status?name=ryan'));
```

The following output is produced:

```
1    {
2      href: '/status?name=ryan',
3      search: '?name=ryan',
4      query: 'name=ryan',
5      pathname: '/status'
6    }
```

The processing of Querystring can take place in a further step:

```
1    var url = require('url');
2    console.log(url.parse('/status?name=ryan', true));
```

The following output is produced:

```
1    {
2      href: '/status?name=ryan',
3      search: '?name=ryan',
4      query: { name: 'ryan' },
5      pathname: '/status'
6    }
```

The status code, which is used during the answer of the messages, stands in `message.statusCode`. The suitable text for that can be found in `message.statusMessage`. The code is three-figure HTTP code, e.g., 404. This value is only reachable if the object comes from `http.ClientRequest`.

By means of `message.socket` access to `net.Socket` objects exists, which is assigned to the used connection.

HTTPS

HTTPS is HTTP, which continues on TLS (Transport Layer Security). The actual TLS version corresponds to the earlier standard SSL 3.0. TSL is the successor of SSL.

If HTTPS is used, then you can determine the authentication data of the clients with: request.connection.verifyPeer() and request.connection.getPeerCertificate().

The server is provided as follows with HTTP:

`https.createServer(options[, requestListener])`

```
1   // Abruf: https://localhost:8000/
2   var https = require('https');
3   var fs = require('fs');
4
5   var options = {
6     key: fs.readFileSync('test/fixtures/keys/agent2-key.pem'),
7     cert: fs.readFileSync('test/fixtures/keys/agent2-cert.pem')
8   };
9
10  https.createServer(options, function (req, res) {
11    res.writeHead(200);
12    res.end("hello world\n");
13  }).listen(8000);
14  Or
15
16  var https = require('https');
17  var fs = require('fs');
18
19  var options = {
20    pfx: fs.readFileSync('server.pfx')
21  };
22
23  https.createServer(options, function (req, res) {
24    res.writeHead(200);
25    res.end("hello world\n");
26  }).listen(8000);
```

The used methods and features resemble to a large extent those of the module http:

```
1   var https = require('https');
2
3   var options = {
4     hostname: 'encrypted.google.com',
5     port: 443,
6     path: '/',
7     method: 'GET'
8   };
9
10  var req = https.request(options, function(res) {
11    console.log("statusCode: ", res.statusCode);
```

```
12    console.log("headers: ", res.headers);
13
14    res.on('data', function(d) {
15       process.stdout.write(d);
16    });
17  });
18  req.end();
19
20  req.on('error', function(e) {
21    console.error(e);
22  });
```

The argument *options* has further options, unlike "HTTP":

- pfx: certificates, private keys and information of the certificate authority (CA). The default value is "null".

- key: the private key. The default value is "null".

- passphrase: the pass phrase for the private key. The default value is "null".

- cert: public x509 certificate. The default value is "null".

- ca: an array of certificate authority, which are inquired, in order to dissolve the host

- ciphers: a character string which merges or excludes the used ciphers. See OpenSSL[2] to take a look at how this is designed.

- rejectUnauthorized: If true, the certificate will be checked about its certificate authority. An error even arises if the examination fails. The default value is true. You should switch this off in test environments if necessary. This examination takes place on the level of the connection establishment, before the HTTP request was sent.

- secureProtocol: the method, for example *TLSv1*. Available methods stand in "SSL_METHODS".

```
1  var options = {
2    hostname: 'encrypted.google.com',
3    port: 443,
4    path: '/',
5    method: 'GET',
6    key: fs.readFileSync('test/fixtures/keys/agent2-key.pem'),
7    cert: fs.readFileSync('test/fixtures/keys/agent2-cert.pem')
8  };
9  options.agent = new https.Agent(options);
10
11  var req = https.request(options, function(res) {
12  ...
13  }
```

---

[2]http://www.openssl.org/docs/apps/ciphers.html#CIPHER_LIST_FORMAT

You can also this without an "agent" object.

```
1   var options = {
2     hostname: 'encrypted.google.com',
3     port: 443,
4     path: '/',
5     method: 'GET',
6     key: fs.readFileSync('test/fixtures/keys/agent2-key.pem'),
7     cert: fs.readFileSync('test/fixtures/keys/agent2-cert.pem'),
8     agent: false
9   };
10
11  var req = https.request(options, function(res) {
12    ...
13  }
```

Handling Files and Paths

Node can access files directly over the appropriate modules and all typical operations on these files as well as on paths and folders.

Access to the File System

The file system access under Node is made available by the module *fs*. All calls can take place both synchronously and asynchronously. While for client page scripts (in principle only asynchronous) one of the calls is meaningful, this can be regarded on the server somewhat differently. Since the result of an action is possibly sending JSON or HTML, one usually waits anyway, until the result is present. Asynchronous calls do not have an advantage. However, if your environment is strongly burdening and scripts have noticeable running times, then Node will only always work on a request and then all synchronous actions for these will occur. All other requests wait. Now, if a script waits substantially for a file operation for this part, then the process is altogether slowed down.

⚲ Synchronously or Asynchronously   You rarely do something wrong with asynchronous calls, even if no noticeable effect arises. Program always asynchronously, unless there are good reasons to do it differently and you know the results that will happen from it.

Asynchronous calls always use a callback function as last argument. The callback functions have different signatures. However, it is common that the first argument of the callback function is an exception object (exception), which shows errors. In case of success, this object is undefined or "null," so that a simple test with if(!exception) can start.

Synchronous calls always produce an immediate exception. If an error arises, use try/catch for treating the error conditions.

Here is a first example of the asynchronous use:

```
1   var fs = require('fs');
2
3   fs.unlink('/tmp/hello', function (err) {
4     if (err) throw err;
5     console.log('successfully deleted /tmp/hello');
6   });
```

Here, the same example of the synchronous use (consider the suffix *Sync* in line 3):

```
1   var fs = require('fs');
2
3   fs.unlinkSync('/tmp/hello');
4   console.log('successfully deleted /tmp/hello');
```

Asynchronous calls don't return in deterministic time. If you start several calls, the sequence is not guaranteed with the return. The following example is therefore error-prone:

```
1   fs.rename('/tmp/hello', '/tmp/world', function (err) {
2     if (err) throw err;
3     console.log('renamed complete');
4   });
5   fs.stat('/tmp/world', function (err, stats) {
6     if (err) throw err;
7     console.log('stats: ' + JSON.stringify(stats));
8   });
```

Here it can happen that the call of fs.stat in line 5 is successful, before the renaming in line one with "fs.rename" has been finished. Therefore, you should concatenate several asynchronous calls that connect with each other:

```
1   fs.rename('/tmp/hello', '/tmp/world', function (err) {
2     if (err) throw err;
3     fs.stat('/tmp/world', function (err, stats) {
4       if (err) throw err;
5       console.log('stats: ' + JSON.stringify(stats));
6     });
7   });
```

You can work with absolute or relative paths. If you work with relative paths, it should be clear that the origin of the current listing is the process in which the script is implemented. This can be determined with process.cwd(). Usually this is Node core.

Sometimes it can occur that you start the action, but don't need the result. Then you can omit the callback function. But if an error occurs now, the entrance to the exception object will be missing. In order to arrive nevertheless at this error message, you use the environment variable NODE_DEBUG. The following script shows how this takes place:

File: script.js

```
1  function bad() {
2     require('fs').readFile('/');
3  }
4  bad();
```

Use the script as follows:

```
1  $ env NODE_DEBUG=fs node script.js
```

The following output occurs:

```
1  fs.js:66
2          throw err;
3                ^
4  Error: EISDIR, read
5      at rethrow (fs.js:61:21)
6      at maybeCallback (fs.js:79:42)
7      at Object.fs.readFile (fs.js:153:18)
8      at bad (/path/to/script.js:2:17)
9      at Object.<anonymous> (/path/to/script.js:5:1)
10     <etc.>
```

This certainly only succeeds if the path cannot really be read. In the example, the root "/" is accessed.

Functions for the File Access

This section shows the most important file access functions. Here, only the asynchronous methods are shown. Most methods also exist synchronously. They then have the suffix "Sync" in the name ("rename" versus "renameSync"). With the synchronous methods, the callback function is void.

fs.rename(oldPath, newPath, callback) renames a file. With fs.ftruncate(fd, len, callback), you empty a file. Either a file description object or a path for the file is used for this.

The function group fs.fchown(fd, uid, gid, callback) and fs.lchown(path, uid, gid, callback) sets the owner of a file. Either a file description object is used or the path for the file. The group fs.fchown(fd, mode, callback), fs.chown(path, mode, callback) sets rights to a file. Either a file description object is used or the path for the file.

 These functions are applicable only on Unix systems.

 On Windows you now use the function *icals* if the setting of rights is necessary, which you can access in the Windows command line, e.g., as follows: icacls onlyread.txt /inheritance:r/grant %username%:r

---

With fs.fstat(fd, callback), fs.stat(path, callback), or fs.lstat(path, callback), you determine information about a file. The callback function has two arguments: *err* and *stats*. *stats* is of the type fs.Stats. lstat processes the link if it's a symbolic link, not the goal of the link.

With fs.realpath(path[, cache], callback), you determine the genuine path of a file.

```
1  var cache = {'/etc':'/private/etc'};
2  fs.realpath('/etc/passwd', cache, function (err, resolvedPath) {
3    if (err) throw err;
4    console.log(resolvedPath);
5  });
```

The method fs.unlink(path, callback) deletes a file. With fs.rmdir(path, callback), a folder is removed. The callback function does not have additional arguments.

With fs.mkdir(path[,mode],callback), a folder is produced. That access to the folder is specified with 0777 (all to have all rights).

fs.readdir(path, callback) serves to read a folder and place all files in there as an array. The special folders "." and ".." are not taken up.

The method fs.close(fd, callback) closes an opened file. The callback function does not have additional arguments. fs.open(path, flags[,mode], callback) opens a file for access. The argument *flags* has the following meaning:

- "r": open for reading. An exception releases if the file cannot be opened.

- "r+": open for reading and writing. An exception releases if the file cannot be opened or described.

- "rs": opens for synchronous access and by avoidance local caches. This can be meaningful with external storage systems; however, it affects the performance negatively.

- "rs+": opens for synchronous writable access and by avoidance local Caches. This can be meaningful with external storage systems; however, it affects the peformance negatively.

- "w": opens for writing and if the file does not exist, it is produced. If it exists, it is emptied.

- "wx": opens for writing and, if the file exists, an exception is produced

- "w+" opens for reading and writing. If the file does not exist, it is produced. If it exists, it is emptied.

- "wx+" opens for reading and writing. If the file exists, an exception is produced.

- "a": opens for writing and, if the file exists, new data is attached

- "ax": opens for writing and, if the file exists, an exception is released

- "a+": opens for reading and writing and, if the file exists, new data is attached

- "ax+": opens for reading and writing and, if the file exists, an exception is released

mode sets the right of access, if the file is produced. The default value is 0666, writing and reading.

The timestamp of a file can be changed with fs.utimes(path, atime, mtime, callback) and/or with fs.futimes(fd, atime, mtime, callback).

The writing of data happens with fs.write(fd, buffer, offset, length[,position], callback). *buffer* delivers bites, *position* the position yet to be.

written is *offset*, the position in the buffer. The callback function indicates the written bytes, once the number and the buffer. Alternatively fs.write(fd, data[, position[, encoding]], callback) is used.

Reading from data takes place with a description object *fd* by the means of fs.read(fd, buffer, offset, length, position, callback):

- *buffer* is the buffer, where the data is written.

- *offset* is the starting point of the buffer.

- *length* is the amount of the readable bytes.

- *position* is the position in the file.

The callback function indicates the number of really read bytes and the buffer.
Directly works with a file with fs.readFile(filename[,options], callback).

```
1   fs.readFile('/etc/passwd', function (err, data) {
2     if (err) throw err;
3     console.log(data);
4   });
```

The writing to a file takes place with fs.writeFile(filename, data[,options],callback).

```
1   fs.writeFile('message.txt', 'Hello Node', function (err) {
2     if (err) throw err;
3     console.log('It\'s saved!');
4   });
```

With fs.appendFile(filename, data[,options],callback) it will be attached directly to existing files.

```
1   fs.appendFile('message.txt', 'data to append',
2                 function (err) {
3     if (err) throw err;
4       console.log('The "data to append" was appended to file!');
5   });
```

The method fs.watch(filename[,options][,listener] serves to supervise a file during the process of renaming. The method returns an instance of the type fs.FSWatcher.

 Platform Dependence   This method is not available on all platforms. It uses operating system functions, which differ slightly:

- Linux uses *inotify.*

- BSD uses *kqueue.*

- OS X uses *kqueue* for files and *FSEvents* for folders.

- Windows uses *ReadDirectoryChangesW* (Win32 API).

```
1   fs.watch('somedir', function (event, filename) {
2     console.log('event is: ' + event);
3     if (filename) {
4       console.log('filename provided: ' + filename);
5     } else {
6       console.log('filename not provided');
7     }
8   });
```

There is a method fs.exists(path, callback), which tests if the file exists. However, the use of this is not recommended.

⚠ **Caution with Test Functions**   Node is a multi-user environment. If a process deletes files and another tests them, then the processes can overlap in such a way that the deletion takes place immediately after the test with "exists" starts. Then the process of the code suggests that the file is present, which is not the case. This is not controllable and leads to so-called "race conditions"—[Race Conditions] (https://de.wikipedia. org/wiki/Race_Condition). It is better if you directly access the file and treat errors with "try/catch" blocks.

With fs.access(path[, mode], callback), you test the rights of access for the current user. The return contains values from a list of constants:

- fs.F_OK: The file is visibile. It says nothing about the rights.

- fs.R_OK: readable

- fs.W_OK: writable

- fs.X_OK: executable

```
1   fs.access('/etc/passwd', fs.R_OK | fs.W_OK, function(err) {
2     util.debug(err ? 'no access!' : 'can read/write');
3   });
```

Functions for handling Streams

Streams process data byte by byte, which usually is more efficient.

ℹ **Streams**   Streams are a paradigm in programming. They make data available as sequence during one period. More to the theory can be found on Wikipedia.[3]

---

[3]https://en.wikipedia.org/wiki/Stream_(computing)

The call fs.createReadStream(path[, options]) returns a ReadStream object. The argument *options* has these default values:

```
1  {
2    flags: 'r',
3    encoding: null,
4    fd: null,
5    mode: 0666,
6    autoClose: true
7  }
```

```
1  fs.createReadStream('sample.txt', {start: 90, end: 99});
```

With fs.createWriteStream(path[,options]), a stream to write is provided. The object is of the type WriteStream.

```
1  {
2    flags: 'w',
3    encoding: null,
4    fd: null,
5    mode: 0666
6  }
```

CHAPTER 5

Introduction to Express

Express is the middleware component of a Node application. Thus, the switching layer between the client and the back end is meant with its persistence functions. The core task is the routing.

Installation

A condition for Express is a functioning Node environment. If this is available, you can create your first application. The operational sequence shown here makes Express available; however, you must provide the actual infrastructure manually. In the section ** application structure **, you find information about how the express generator can be used in order to simplify this.

First, a folder for the application is created:

```
1    mkdir SimpleApp
2    cd SimpleApp
```

With "nmp init", you then produce a *package.json* file. Thus, the application and its dependence are described.

```
1    npm init
```

The information for the description file is queried in the dialogue. In most cases it is to be transferred to order the standards. Thus, simply press ENTER several times, except for the option "entry point." Here you enter the following:

```
1    entry point: app.js
```

This determines that the starting file, thus the beginning of the application, is *app.js*. You can naturally select each name.

Now Express is being installed and received in the list of dependence (option "-save"). If necessary, add the option -g to make Express globally available. That is meaningful, if you plan on developing further proects with Node.

```
1    $ npm install express --save
```

© Jörg Krause 2017

J. Krause, *Programming Web Applications with Node, Express and Pug*, DOI 10.1007/978-1-4842-2511-0_5

```
joerg@joerg-DevMachine: ~/Apps/Jade
Press ^C at any time to quit.
name: (Jade)
version: (0.0.0)
description: Jade Installation
entry point: (index.js)
test command:
git repository:
keywords:
author: Joerg
license: (BSD-2-Clause)
About to write to /home/joerg/Apps/Jade/package.json:

{
  "name": "Jade",
  "version": "0.0.0",
  "description": "Jade Installation ",
  "main": "index.js",
  "scripts": {
    "test": "echo \"Error: no test specified\" && exit 1"
  },
  "author": "Joerg",
  "license": "BSD-2-Clause"
}

Is this ok? (yes)
```

Figure 5-1. *Interactive installation (Ubuntu)*

Application structure

Express supplies a finished application structure. With the installation, not only is the Express module available, but also the finished folder structure can be provided with only one instruction.

However, you do not have to use this. It is quite possible to provide an application very easily by only constructing one file.

With the installation in the previous section, it was said during the initialization that the starting file is named *app.js*. However, this could now look as follows:

```
1   var express = require('express');
2   var app = express();
3
4   app.get('/', function (req, res) {
5     res.send('Hallo Express!');
6   });
7
8   var server = app.listen(3000, function () {
9     var host = server.address().address;
10    var port = server.address().port;
11
12    console.log('I listen on http://%s:%s', host, port);
13  });
```

Here Express is first merged and provides with the constructor call an application *App*. Then a route is specified, the master route "/". All other calls lead to an HTTP error 404 (not found). Then the terminal is determined, here the port 3000 on the local system (line 8). Now if an HTTP request arrives, the function of the suitable route is implemented. In the example the text "hello express!" is spent afterwards. HTML does not return this script. Everything must be settled separately. However, it already concerns a correct HTML communication.

The express generator

For producing an application, the express generator can be used. This is available as a further NPM package.

```
1   $ npm install express-generator -g
```

In addition, the generator has some options, but also produces a meaningful environment without further details.

Table 5-1. *Options of the express generators*

Option	Meaning
–version	Version
–pug	Pug Engine support
-e, –ejs	EJS-Engine (see www.embeddedjs.com)
-hbs	Handlebars Engine
-H, –hogan	Hogan Engine (www.hogan.js)
-c, –css [CS]	CSS Precompiler
-f, –force	Force files in nonempty folders

The standard Template engine is Jade.

The CSS Precompiler can be one of the following (name and, in parentheses, the one which can be used as option):

- LESS (less)

- Stylus (stylus)

- Compass (compass)

- SASS (sass)

Without information, simple CSS is expected.

LESS or SASS

In this work, LESS (*http://lesscss.org*) is used. That is, in principle irrelevant. If you already have a favorite, use that one. If both are new, then you might become somewhat happier with LESS at the beginning, since it is simpler and more common (more sources for learning and less expenditure). However, most professionals use SASS instead (*http://sass-lang.com*).

The generator also produces the master directory of the application, so that you should begin in the superordinate listing:

```
1   express PortalApp
2   cd PortalApp
3   npm install
```

With this instruction sequence, an application with the name *PortalApp* is provided in the folder *PortalApp*. Now the application is started in the Debug mode:

```
set DEBUG=PortalApp & npm start
```

The standard address is *http://localhost:3000*. The web server is based on Node and further settings at the operating system are not necessary. You must neither have ISS nor Apache nor any other server available for this. It just functions.

⚠ **Windows**   Under Windows Sockets for HTTP, communication from the Kernel driver http.sys are made available. Node registers the Port 3000 there. That succeeds only if the port is free. Thus it can happen that Node collides with a likewise installed and active IIS or Apache web server.

🔑 **Only for the start**   It is smart to begin with the structure produced by the generator and start with further modifications at a later time if the need for it is there.

The following structure develops according to standard:

Figure 5-2. *Structure, which the generator puts on*

Routing in Node application

The Routing manufactures a connection between a URL and an implementing instance (method or module). Every time an application delivers more than one site, routing comes into play. That also applies to Single Page Applications (SPA). Because with the conditions of today's browsers you are well advised if everything is pressed into only one site. The rough raster of the application is waved better in several server page modules, which can be implemented well for their part in each case as SPA.

This has a completely different meaning if no SPA is provided. Then it's practically about steering the distribution of each single page. Apart from the sites themselves, the routing then also deals with the parameters, which are provided as part of the URL and which must be supplied with implementing methods.

Routing in Express

If more sites of an application are added, more routes are needed. In addition, serves the express router. This will be more comprehensively treated later on. However, routes do not only deliver finished sites. If a part of the application in the Single Page Style (SPA) is developed, use Express in order to provide the routes for their client page programmed calls. For example, this can take place with AngularJS. Express then illustrates a RESTful back end for AngularJS.

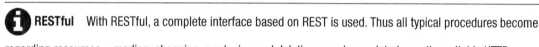 **RESTful** With RESTful, a complete interface based on REST is used. Thus all typical procedures become regarding resources—reading, changing, producing and deleting—and completed over the suitable HTTP instructions.

Only the combination of server page technology and client page elements constitutes a modern Web application.

The Express Router

The Express Router is a pure routing module without many extras.

There is no explicit support of Views or pre-defined settings. However, there are rudimentary APIs like use(), get(), param() and route(). There are different possibilities of using the router. The use of get() is thereby only one variant. The following example application uses these and some other techniques. At the end of the text you'll find a complete description of the entire API.

 API API stands for *Application Programming Interface* and designates a clearly defined interface, over which applications can access functions of a library or a framework.

An example application

The example application has some techniques, which can be used meaningfully in practice:

- simple routes, e.g., to the homepage
- sectional routes, e.g., for the Admin range

- use of the middleware for the logging

- use of parameters

- use of the middleware for the validation of parameters

- implementation of a registration function with distinction of GET and POST

- validation of a parameter for a certain route

Now, the term middleware has already been used several times. But why is it called that and where is the connection with Express?

Middleware – the mediator layer

The name middleware is splendidly selected. The functions placed here are implemented after the arrival of the request by the client and before the forwarding of an answer. Thus, they have relevant influence on the processing of the request. An application is the logging of requests. These take place in the middleware, without consideration for the function of the other components. They are transparent and in the background.

 Middleware   Middleware (service layer or intermediate's application) designates application-neutral

programs, which mediate between applications in order to hide the complexity of these applications and their infrastructure in computer science. One can view middleware as a kind distribution platform. A middleware supports communication between processes. In Express, the middleware is the meditator between request and answer.

Basic routes

The route to the home page was already defined. These, like all other routes, are defined in the file *app.js*. This file is in the best place in the project, as long as the number of routes is visible. Since with a Single Page Application (SPA) only the rough raster of the routes is used on the sever, this is correct. AngularJS then deals with the routes on the client site and regulates the inquiry-specific partial sighting by means of parameters.

Defined routes react to specific paths and HTTP verbs such as GET, POST, PUT/PATCH or DELETE. This functions—with or without RESTful actions—as long as only one handful of routes is needed.

Now it can occur that nevertheless more complex routes become necessary. Complex web sites have not only a range, but also back-end functions, administration ranges, import and export, reporting, and much more. Each range can have innumerable routes.

Simplification of the examples   The following examples only send simple data back instead of

complete Views, in order to arrange the code more readably. Replace the returns through appropriate View calls in practice. The starting point is the function `express.Router()`.

The function `express.Router()` is a kind of mini-application. You thereby produce an instance of the router and define for this instance some routes.

Listing 5-1. app.js

```
1    // Die Applikationsinstanz wird gebildet
2    var express = require('express');
3    var app = express();
4
5    // Eine neue Instanz des Routers wird erstellt
6    var adminRouter = express.Router();
7
8    // The Admin-Site (http://localhost:3000/admin)
9    adminRouter.get('/', function(req, res) {
10     res.send('Homepage of admin area!');
11   });
12
13   // The User-Site (http://localhost:3000/admin/users)
14   adminRouter.get('/users', function(req, res) {
15     res.send('show all users!');
16   });
17
18   // The article-Seite (http://localhost:3000/admin/article)
19   adminRouter.get('/article', function(req, res) {
20     res.send('Show all articles!');
21   });
22
23   // Assign routes to application
24   app.use('/admin', adminRouter);
25
26   // Der Server
27   var server = app.listen(3000, function() {
28     console.log('Server started');
29   });
```

The routes are basically provided in an isolated manner and then assigned as a group of the application. Thereby, the paths are added.

The master path is determined by the method "use." The instruction could also look as follows:

```
app.use('/app', router)
```

Such mini-applications can be assigned several times and thus can win you some clarity over things. Logically separate ranges, as for example Views and REST API, can be kept apart now and can cleanly be separated in the source code.

The Router Middleware (router.use())

The middleware generally intervenes *before* the actual processing.

This is meaningful for a set of tasks:

- authentication
- authorization
- logging
- cache

Q **Infrastructure use!** Above all, tasks like the authentication should never take place in the password, but take off from the infrastructure.

The definition of the functions takes place in the same order in which it is supposed to be used later on. The facility takes place after the production of the application before assigning the routes. The following example shows how all requests on the console are spent.

```
1  // Funktion, die auf jede Anfrage reagiert
2  adminRouter.use(function(req, res, next) {
3    // Konsolenausgabe
4    console.log(req.method, req.url);
5    // Weiter mit der regulären Verarbeitung
6    next();
7  });
```

The call of the method next() is crucial. Therewith, Express is being told that the method was processed and the regular processing can continue. adminRouter.use() defines the middleware function. Actual functionality is to be separately implemented and thus pure JavaScript.

The sequence of the registration of the functions also determines the order of the processing. After the route there is no place for the middleware functions, because the processing of the request ends there with the sending of the data.

Structure Routes

So far it was already shown how routes can be assigned in sections.

The approach is similar with most projects. The home page with its most important link is a range, the administration another. An API—RESTful or not—should always be led separately. Thus, you have enough clearance in order not to lose the overwie with extensions.

The definition of the ranges then looks like this:

```
1  app.use('/', basicRoutes);
2  app.use('/admin', adminRoutes);
3  app.use('/api', apiRoutes);
```

Routes with Parameters (/hello/:id)

The call of a site alone is usually not sufficient. If data from databases is called up, parameters must be transferred. The structure of the URL is almost arbitrary. However, they must consider the borders of HTTP. A URL is limited on 2000 indications. In addition, a complex URL makes you want to play with it, as it's clearly visible and easy to manipulate. The more complex the URL, the more highly is the expenditure for the validation of the parameters.

If you call data up from databases, it offers to limit the primary key for all calls. That leads the data in the business logic to it (from connected tables or documents); thus, they'll possibly be loaded again. In delivering such requests, databases are very good and the simplification with the organization of the server code is nearly never more valuable. Always call their primary parameter *id*.

In the description of the route, parameters are introduced with a colon:

```
1  adminRouter.get('/users/:id', function(req, res) {
2    res.send('Benutzer-ID: ' + req.params.id + '!');
3  });
```

The router recognizes this and transfers the values into an object with the name *params*, which is part of the requirement object *req*.

There, the parameters are available as features. The URL for this example looks as follows:

http://localhost:3000/admin/users/123

The path section *admin* was defined in the router. The specific path specifies *user* and *123* to the feature *id* to hand over. The colon serves the recognition and is not part of the path.

Because of the high susceptibility for manupulations, parameters must always be validated. Here again the middleware layer comes into play. It makes a method called param() available, to which the parameters are handed over before they are supplied to the processing.

Router Middleware for Parameters (.param)

Parameters must always be validated by high susceptibility for manipulations. Here again the middleware layer comes into play. It makes a method called param(), to which the parameters are handed over, before they are supplied to the processing.

The following example shows how the parameter *id* is checked:

Listing 5-2. param_sample.js

```
1   adminRouter.param('id', function(req, res, next, name) {
2     console.log('Validierung für ID ' + id);
3     var id = Number(req.params.id);
4     if (!id){
5       // Fehlerbehandlung
6     } else {
7       // Ablage des geprüften Wertes
8       req.id = id;
9       // Weiter mit Verarbeitung
10      next();
11    }
12  });

14  adminRouter.get('/users/:id', function(req, res) {
15    res.send('ID: ' + req.id + '!');
16  });
```

A valid URL is here:

http://localhost:3000/admin/users/123

How the error handling looks here depends on the setting of tasks. A web site for (human) users requires reliably different reactions than a RESTful API, which must possibly react to technical errors.

Several Routes (app.route())

The function app.route() is a direct call of the router and corresponds to the call express.Router(). However, the function has in addition the possibility to create more routes in one step and to provide several actions over only one route. The latter avoids that with hundreds of actions. Likewise, many routes must be provided.

In the following example, a /login route is defined. To these react two methods: once the Verb GET is evaluated, once POST.

Listing 5-3. login_sample.js

```
1   app.route('/login')
2       .get(function(req, res) {
3           res.send('Das Anmeldeformular.');
4       })
5       .post(function(req, res) {
6           console.log('Anmelden');
7           res.send('Anmeldung verarbeitet!');
8       });
```

app is in this example the central application object and the definition usually takes place in the *app.js* file.

The approach is typical for all kinds of forms. If the page in the browser with *http://localhost:3000/login* is called, the browser produces a GET request. The user sees the form and fills it out. It sends it then with the transmission button (submit). The browser now provides a POST request and adds the form data.

ℹ **Where is the HTML?** In the example, the necessary HTML is not shown in order to keep the listing small. Simply write the standard form with HTML. There are no features for the processing with express.

One may now speak of the actions of a route. In the last example there were two actions. A RESTful API could react to further Verbs with the same route.

CHAPTER 6

Introduction to Pug

Pug is a template engine for Express, the middleware and routing solution for Node.js. It is the standard for Express. If you argue intensively with Node.js and Express, no way leads past *Pug*.

Overview

Pug uses a simplified representation of the HTML site by simple text instructions. These correspond in a practical way to the names of the HTML tags. Since HTML develops a hierarchy and *Pug* knows no closing tag, the tree structure must develop differently. In addition, *Pug* uses identations in the text editor. 2 blanks show that the following element is a child element.

 Editor configuration   For *Pug* to function, you must adjust the text editor to an indentation by the TAB key by 2 indentations.

Preparation

Pug presupposes that you work with *node.js* and use the middleware *Express*. The simplest way to a functioning environment goes over gradual processing of the components of a node.js installation. This was described already in the previous chapters. If the environment consists of Node and Express, the occupation with *Pug* has nothing more in its way.

© Jörg Krause 2017
J. Krause, *Programming Web Applications with Node, Express and Pug*, DOI 10.1007/978-1-4842-2511-0_6

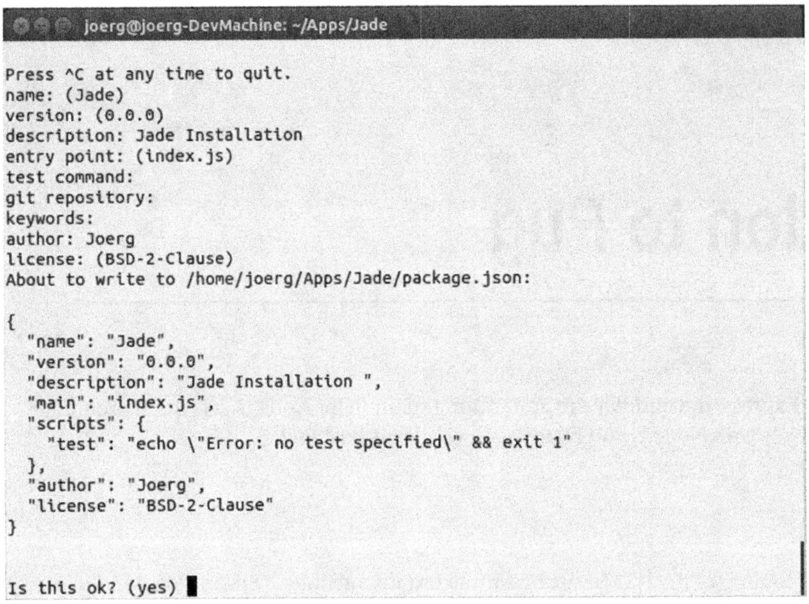

```
joerg@joerg-DevMachine: ~/Apps/Jade

Press ^C at any time to quit.
name: (Jade)
version: (0.0.0)
description: Jade Installation
entry point: (index.js)
test command:
git repository:
keywords:
author: Joerg
license: (BSD-2-Clause)
About to write to /home/joerg/Apps/Jade/package.json:

{
  "name": "Jade",
  "version": "0.0.0",
  "description": "Jade Installation ",
  "main": "index.js",
  "scripts": {
    "test": "echo \"Error: no test specified\" && exit 1"
  },
  "author": "Joerg",
  "license": "BSD-2-Clause"
}

Is this ok? (yes)
```

Figure 6-1. Description of the application

Place a file with a name similar to *index.js* in the newly created listing application. It has the following contents:

```
1   var express = require('express');
2   var app = express();
3
4   app.get('/', function (req, res) {
5     res.send('Hello Express!');
6   });
7
8   var server = app.listen(3000, function () {});
```

Now start the Node server:

```
1   npm start
```

```
joerg@JoergDev:~/Apps/WebAppsNode/portalapp$ npm start

> portalapp@0.0.0 start /home/joerg/Apps/WebAppsNode/portalapp
> node ./bin/www
```

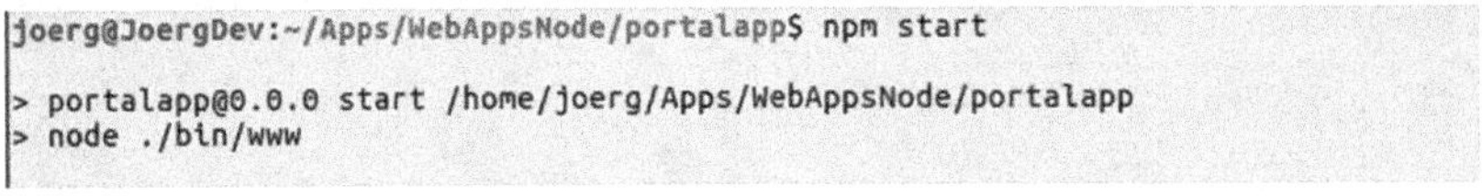

Figure 6-2. Start the application

Now enter the following URL in the development system of your browser: *http://localhost:3000*. You should then see the "Hello Express!" output.

Figure 6-3. *Output of the page*

Application structure

Express offers a number of exciting functions. However, here I want to only deal with *Pug* and therefore the manual producing and use of a view is simpler.

The simplest use of *Pug* consists of two components. On the one hand the first View, *index.pug*:

File: index.pug

```
1   doctype html
2   html(lang='en')
3     head
4       title= title
5     body!= body
6       h1= title
```

On the other hand the "Hello Express" example is changed in such a way that now instead of the static text, the View is used (and text reads "Hello Pug"):

File: index.js

```
1   var express = require('express');
2   var app = express();
3   app.set('view engine', 'pug');
4
5   app.get('/', function (req, res) {
6     res.render('index', {
7       title: 'Hello Pug!'
8     });
9   });
10
11  var server = app.listen(3000, function () {});
```

On the other hand *Pug* is agreed as standard, by which no file extensions must be indicated and the suitable module is first loaded.

This happens through:

```
app.set('view engine', 'pug');
```

Then instead of res_send, the function res_render is used. The first parameter is the name of the View, which can be indicated without a path (according to standard, it will be searched in *view* files) and without file extension (according to standard now, *pug* is used). The second parameter is an object that the local variable intends for the View. Each characteristic of the object is made available as the local variable. In the example, that is the value of *title*.

Pug views

Instead of HTML, you now write the viewable sites in pug. Again, the just-used example:

File: index.pug

```
1    doctype html
2    html(lang='en')
3      head
4        title= title
5      body!= body
6        h1= title
```

On each line of the View, an HTML tag has to be there first. Instead of spelling in XML form ('<title></title>'), *Pug* takes place as simplfied representation here.

```
title= title
```

The left part is the HTML element. An equal sign follows, which determines the coding and thus the treatment of HTML-specific entities such as "<" or ">". Then JavaScript follows. Since a local variable with the name title was agreed upon, this expression is written down here. Similarly, it functions with h1, which stands underneath the body element. Handling body aims at the fact that Views (layout or master sites) is usually assigned to the variable body (right in the expression) on content sites. Since HTML is supposed to be taken over directly by one site, the operator ! = will be used but not coded.

Figure 6-4. *Output of the view*

Handling Partial Views

Partial Views permit a structuring of Views. One *Pug* View looks, for example, as follows:

File: index.pug

```
1    doctype html
2    html(lang='en')
3      head
4        title= title
5      body!= body
6        include navigation
7        h1= title
```

With the instruction include a further View is merged, *navigation.pug*. Note that this is indicated without quotation marks and clips.

Now this navigation is provided in a further file: *views/navigation.pug*:

File: navigation.pug

```
1    div#navigation
2      a(href='/') home
```

home

Hello Pug!

Figure 6-5. *Output of script*

Handling Layout Pages

A layout page is a master whose contents are determined by contents pages. That corresponds to the layout page in ASP.NET MVC or the master page in ASP.NET.

As example, a layout page can look as follows:

File: index.pug

```
1    doctype html
2    html(lang='en')
3      head
4        title= title
5      body!= body
6        block content
7        include navigation
```

This hardly differs from the previous example. Only the "h1" element in the end is missing.

file: content.pug

```
1   extends index
2
3   block content
4     h1= title
5     a(href='http://www.joergkrause.de/') Jörg &lt;Is A Geek&gt; Krause
```

It refers to the layout page. Now the starting script is adapted, because *Pug* renders the contents site first, which calls the layout site for its part.

file: index.js

```
1    var express = require('express');
2    var app = express();
3    app.set('view engine', 'pug');
4
5    app.get('/', function (req, res) {
6      res.render('content', {
7        title: 'Hallo Pug!'
8      });
9    });
10
11   var server = app.listen(3000, function () {});
```

Keep the "res.render" function in mind, which now calls *content* instead of *index* (line 5).
Now the node server can be started (in the folder where the file *package.json* stands):

npm start

As long as the standard port was not assigned somewhere else, the browser shows the rendered HTML site now:

http://127.0.0.1:3000/

The entry point is the call of *res.render* with the argument of the contents site, *content.pug*. Then the engine provides for the shop of the layout site and the processing. Thus, the entire procedure takes place on the server:

Figure 6-6. *Output with layout site*

It is noticeable that the navigation disappeared. That is the normal behavior. Because now contents of the body element were actually supplied by a contents page and therefore the static contents are overwritten. Certainly there are some options here to change this behavior. This is described exactly in the language reference.

CHAPTER 7

■ ■ ■

Language Components of Pug

In the following, you find a systematic language overview. The entrance to the available online information can be found on [Github] (`https://github.com/Pugjs/Pug`).

Doctype

The typical HTML 5 Doctype is written as follows:

```
1   doctype html
```

The produced HTML then looks as follows:

```
1   <!DOCTYPE html>
```

Short Spellings

Because of the frequent use of Doctypes there are a few short spellings.

```
1   doctype html
```

The produced HTML then looks as follows:

```
1   <!DOCTYPE html>
1   doctype xml
```

The produced HTML then looks as follows:

```
1   <?xml version="1.0" encoding="utf-8" ?>
```

```
1   doctype transitional
```

The produced HTML then looks as follows:

```
1   <!DOCTYPE html PUBLIC "-//W3C//DTD XHTML 1.0 Transitional//EN" "http\
2   ://www.w3.org/TR/xhtml1/DTD/xhtml1-transitional.dtd">
```

```
1   doctype strict
```

© Jörg Krause 2017
J. Krause, *Programming Web Applications with Node, Express and Pug*, DOI 10.1007/978-1-4842-2511-0_7

The produced HTML then looks as follows:

```
1  <!DOCTYPE html PUBLIC "-//W3C//DTD XHTML 1.0 Strict//EN" "http://www\
2  .w3.org/TR/xhtml1/DTD/xhtml1-strict.dtd">
```

```
1  doctype frameset
```

The produced HTML then looks as follows:

```
1  <!DOCTYPE html PUBLIC "-//W3C//DTD XHTML 1.0 Frameset//EN" "http://w\
2  ww.w3.org/TR/xhtml1/DTD/xhtml1-frameset.dtd">
```

```
1  doctype 1.1
```

The produced HTML then looks as follows:

```
1  <!DOCTYPE html PUBLIC "-//W3C//DTD XHTML 1.1//EN" "http://www.w3.org\
2  /TR/xhtml11/DTD/xhtml11.dtd">
```

```
1  doctype basic
```

The produced HTML then looks as follows:

```
1  <!DOCTYPE html PUBLIC "-//W3C//DTD XHTML Basic 1.1//EN" "http://www.\
2  w3.org/TR/xhtml-basic/xhtml-basic11.dtd">
```

```
1  doctype mobile
```

The produced HTML then looks as follows:

```
1  <!DOCTYPE html PUBLIC "-//WAPFORUM//DTD XHTML Mobile 1.2//EN" "http:\
2  //www.openmobilealliance.org/tech/DTD/xhtml-mobile12.dtd">
```

Own Doctypes

If deviating Doctypes are necessary, the following syntax can be used:

```
1  doctype html PUBLIC "-//W3C//DTD XHTML Basic 1.1//EN"
```

The following HTML is provided by it:

```
1  <!DOCTYPE html PUBLIC "-//W3C//DTD XHTML Basic 1.1//EN">
```

Options

The Doctypes are not only a source of information for the browser. You should absolutely take the *Pug* version, because these also affect the HTML generator, for example, on handling closing tags.

Here is the direct call of the Renderers with the Doctype "XHTML":

```
1   var pug = require('pug');
2
3   // Translate
4   var fn = pug.compile('img(src="foo.png")',
5                       { doctype: 'xml' });
6
7   // Rendering
8   var html = fn({});
```

The following HTML is provided by it:

```
1   <img src="foo.png"></img>
```

But if HTML is produced, the tag won't be closed:

```
1   // Compilation
2   var fn = pug.compile('img(src="foo.png")',
3                       { doctype: 'html' });
4
5   // Rendering
6   var html = fn({});
```

The following HTML is provided by it:

```
1   <img src="foo.png">
```

Attributes

Attributes look as in HTML; however, the arguments are JavaScript, so that you can simply work dynamically here.

⚠ **Server Side JavaScript**   Note that JavaScript is implemented in arguments on the server and is sending static HTML from the view of the client.

```
1   a(href='google.com') Google
2   a(class='button', href='google.com') Google
```

Translated, this looks as follows:

```
1   <a href="google.com">Google</a><a href="google.com" class="button">G\
2   oogle</a>
```

All usual JavaScript expressions function without problems. They are separated with "-", so that *Pug* won't interpret them as HTML:

```
1    - var authenticated = true
2    body(class=authenticated ? 'auth' : 'anon')
```

Translated, this looks as follows:

```
1    <body class="auth"></body>
```

Several attributes can be divided for the improvement of readableness on several lines:

```
1    input(
2      type='checkbox'
3      name='agreement'
4      checked
5    )
```

Translated to HTML this looks as follows:

```
1    <input type="checkbox" name="agreement" checked="checked"/>
```

Not coded Attribute

According to standard all attributes are coded, i.e., special characters are replaced by appropriate entities ("<" with & gt; and ">" with & it; etc.). With the assignment characters "=" and "!=", the behavior can be steered:

```
1    div(escaped="<code>")
2    div(unescaped!="<code>")
```

In HTML this looks as follows:

```
1    <div escaped="&lt;code&gt;"></div>
2    <div unescaped="<code>"></div>
```

⚠ **Caution!**   It is dangerous with user inputs, which are passed on to sightings in order to turn the coding off. Users can otherwise transfer active code to the server:

Logical Attributes

Logical (boolean) attributes are represented in *Pug* as functions, which can process arguments. For its part, they can either be true or false. If no argument is indicated, the standard is true.

```
1    input(type='checkbox', checked)
2    input(type='checkbox', checked=true)
3    input(type='checkbox', checked=false)
4    input(type='checkbox', checked=true.toString())
```

Translated this looks as follows:

```
1   <input type="checkbox" checked="checked"/>
2   <input type="checkbox" checked="checked"/>
3   <input type="checkbox"/>
4   <input type="checkbox" checked="true"/>
```

If the Doctype of the document is HTML, the shortened attributes are used, as they understand all browsers:

```
1   doctype html
2   input(type='checkbox', checked)
3   input(type='checkbox', checked=true)
4   input(type='checkbox', checked=false)
5   input(type='checkbox', checked=true && 'checked')
```

Translated this looks as follows:

```
1   <!DOCTYPE html>
2   <input type="checkbox" checked>
3   <input type="checkbox" checked>
4   <input type="checkbox">
5   <input type="checkbox" checked="checked">
```

Style Attributes

The `style` attribute is somewhat more complex, because the parameters represent a style object. Contrary to the pure HTML version, which can be read only as character string. *Pug* is here indeed a JSON object.

```
1   a(style={color: 'red', background: 'green'})
```

In HTML this looks as follows:

```
1   <a style="color:red;background:green"></a>
```

ℹ JSON   JSON stands for JavaScript Object Notation. This concerns a compact data format for humans and machine of simply readable text form for the purpose of data exchange between applications. Each valid JSON document should be valid JavaScript. One works on the server and on the client with JavaScript. It acts with JSON basically around the *natural* format for the data transfer and object definition.

& Attributes

This special form, known as "and attributes," is used in order to divide an object into attributes:

```
1   div#foo(data-bar="foo")&attributes({'data-foo': 'bar'})
```

In HTML this turns into:

```
1    <div id="foo" data-bar="foo" data-foo="bar"></div>
```

It must not be object literal. A variable which supplies an object itself is likewise suitable.

```
1    - var attributes = {'data-foo': 'bar'};
2    div#foo(data-bar="foo")&attributes(attributes)
```

Here, the same HTML starts to develop:

```
1    <div id="foo" data-bar="foo" data-foo="bar"></div>
```

 This function does not code HTML. If the data is from a user input, an explicit investigation on embedded codes is necessary. In addition, compare the handling with a mixin, which always takes over coding.

Handling CSS Classes

CSS classes are described by attributes or literals.

The Class Attribute

The class attribute can be used like every other attribute with a character string. Now it occurs frequently that several class names are set. But arrays are also permitted:

```
1    - var classes = ['btn', 'btn-default']
2    a(class=classes)
3    a.bing(class=classes class=['bing'])
```

As shown in line 3, the attribute can be repeated. *Pug* then combines the entries. Subsequently, it becomes the following in HTML:

```
1    <a class="btn btn-default"></a>
2    <a class="btn btn-default bing"></a>
```

If class names are set over conditions, usually a separate logic must be created. In *Pug*, Object Mapping is suitable for this:

```
1    - var curUrl = '/about'
2    a(class={active: curUrl === '/'} href='/') Home
3    a(class={active: curUrl === '/about'} href='/about') Über uns
```

This looks as follows in HTML:

```
1    <a href="/">Home</a>
2    <a href="/about" class="active">Über uns</a>
```

94

The Class Literal

The direct use of the literal one from CSSs is still simpler:

```
1   a.button
```

This looks as follows in HTML:

```
1   <a class="button"></a>
```

A feature with the literal ones is the "<div>" tag. This is the standard, if no element is indicated:

```
1   .content
```

In HTML it turns into the following:

```
1   <div class="content"></div>
```

ID Literal

IDs use the #idname syntax:

```
1   a#main-link
```

This looks as follows in HTML:

```
1   <a id="main-link"></a>
```

Since the "div" element is used very frequently, you can omit it:

```
1   #content
```

In HTML it turns into the following:

```
1   <div id="content"></div>
```

Instructions

Instructions bring interactive sections into the template. They resemble the possibilities of JavaScript, however before the script level is processed. HTML can be embedded directly.

Definition by Cases (case)

case is an instruction for process and corresponds to the switch in JavaScript. The case branches in JavaScript are written as when in *Pug*:

```
1    - var friends = 10
2    case friends
3      when 0
4        p You have no friends
5      when 1
6        p You have one friend
7      default
8        p You have #{friends} friends
```

In HTML it turns into the following:

```
1    <p>You have 10 friends</p>
```

Forwarding to the next Case

Just like in JavaScript, the instruction for the next branch falls through if no instruction follows:

```
1    - var friends = 0
2    case friends
3      when 0
4      when 1
5        p Almost no friends
6      default
7        p You have #{friends} friends
```

In HTML it turns into the following:

```
1    <p>Almost no friends</p>
```

Extension of Blocks

Instead of the spelling of several lines, short texts can be placed on the same line and are then limited on this line:

```
1    - var friends = 1
2    case friends
3      when 0: p You have no friends
4      when 1: p You have one friend
5      default: p You have #{friends} friends
```

The HTML then looks as follows:

```
1    <p>You have one friend</p>
```

Conditions (if)

Conditions are an elementary component in Pug. In relation to JavaScript, the spelling is slightly simplified—so you can omit the clips around the condition.

```
1   - var user = { description: 'Example Text' }
2   - var authorised = false
3   #user
4     if user.description
5       h2 Description
6       p.description= user.description
7     else if authorised
8       h2 Description
9       p.description.
10        User has no description,
11        add one...
12    else
13      h1 Description
14      p.description User has no description
```

The input data then determines which HTML will develop:

```
1   <div id="user">
2     <h2>Description</h2>
3     <p class="description">Example Text</p>
4   </div>
```

The keyword unless remains for negated conditions:

```
1   unless user.isAnonymous
2     p You are logged on as #{user.name}
```

This is perfectly identical to the following expression:

```
1   if !user.isAnonymous
2     p You are logged on as #{user.name}
```

Iterations

With each and while, two possibilities are available to form loops.

each

The use of each is, to a large extent, intuitive:

```
1   ul
2     each val in [1, 2, 3, 4, 5]
3       li= val
```

The HTML is formed on basis of the array on the server:

```
1   <ul>
2     <li>1</li>
3     <li>2</li>
4     <li>3</li>
5     <li>4</li>
6     <li>5</li>
7   </ul>
```

With two parameters, access to the index and the running value exists:

```
1   ul
2     each val, index in ['zero', 'one', 'two']
3       li= index + ': ' + val
```

The HTML shows that the index is based on zero:

```
1   <ul>
2     <li>0: zero</li>
3     <li>1: one</li>
4     <li>2: two</li>
5   </ul>
```

If Hashes (object maps) are used, then index and value can be determined even more exactly:

```
1   ul
2     each val, index in {1:'one',2:'two',3:'three'}
3       li= index + ': ' + val
```

The HTML shows that the index of the source object is certain:

```
1   <ul>
2     <li>1: one</li>
3     <li>2: two</li>
4     <li>3: three</li>
5   </ul>
```

Instead of the direct information, each JavaScript expression can be naturally used, which produces or contains a suitable structure:

```
1   - var values = [];
2   ul
3     each val in values.length ? values : ['No Values']
4       li= val
```

Since the array in the example is empty, the following HTML is produced:

```
1   <ul>
2     <li>No Values</li>
3   </ul>
```

Pseudonym The keyword "for" can be used as alias for "each."

while

A loop with while has a termination condition. The loop keeps going, as long as the expression shows true.

```
1   - var n = 0
2   ul
3     while n < 4
4       li= n++
```

The dynamically produced HTML now looks as follows:

```
1   <ul>
2       <li>0</li>
3       <li>1</li>
4       <li>2</li>
5       <li>3</li>
6   </ul>
```

JavaScript Code

With *Pug*, JavaScript fragments can be written directly into the page.
These parts are then implemented on the server page. Thereby, there are three kinds of code:

Unbuffered Codes

The results when processing are written immediately into the output.

Buffered Codes

The results when processing are written first into a buffer and at the end sent completely to the instruction.

Buffered and not coded Codes

The results when processing are first written into a buffer and sent in the end completely to the instruction. No encoding of the output takes place.

Unbuffered Codes

Unbuffered and also not coded looks as follows:

```
1    - for (var x = 0; x < 3; x++)
2        li item
```

⚠ **Caution!**   As in the preceding examples, you should keep caution during the conversion of user inputs, in order to prevent that such construct code is transferred. The transferred JavaScript code would be implemented in the server page.

In the HTML the following develops from the last example:

```
1    <li>item</li>
2    <li>item</li>
3    <li>item</li>
```

This also functions with blocks (the "-" indication is alone and set off while the following text is compressed):

```
1    -
2      list = ["Uno", "Dos", "Tres",
3              "Cuatro", "Cinco", "Seis"]
4    each item in list
5      li= item
```

Also, this loop generates pure HTML:

```
1    <li>Uno</li>
2    <li>Dos</li>
3    <li>Tres</li>
4    <li>Cuatro</li>
5    <li>Cinco</li>
6    <li>Seis</li>
```

Buffered Code

The buffered part starts indications with a "=" and spends the result of calculation in JavaScript. Here is the coded variant. (You consider the indentation on line 2.):

```
1    p
2      = 'This Code is <coded>!'
```

In HTML, you see how the special characters were converted:

```
1    <p>Dieser Code ist &lt;kodiert&gt;!</p>
```

JavaScript expressions can also begin here:

```
1   p= 'This cvode is' + ' <coded>!'
```

The same result happens as in the previous example:

```
1   <p>This Code is &lt;coded&gt;!</p>
```

Buffered and not coded Codes

The encoding starts again with the "!=" operator. Note that this is not safe regarding data from user inputs.

```
1   p
2     != 'This code is <strong>not</strong> coded!'
```

The following HTML is provided by it:

```
1   <p>This code is <strong>not</strong> coded!
2   </p>
```

Also in this use JavaScript expressions can be used:

```
1   p!= 'This code is' + ' <strong>not</strong> coded!'
```

The following HTML is provided by it:

```
1   <p>This code is <strong>not</strong> coded!</p>
```

Comments

Comments are written just as in JavaScript and then converted into HTML comments, thus not removed completely:

```
1   // Some HTML:
2   p foo
3   p bar
```

The following HTML is provided by it:

```
1   <!-- Some HTML: -->
2   <p>foo</p>
3   <p>bar</p>
```

If somebody puts a line behind the comment symbol, the comment is removed and is not repeated in the HTML:

```
1   //- That's not public
2   p foo
3   p bar
```

The following HTML is provided by it:

```
1   <p>foo</p>
2   <p>bar</p>
```

Comment Blocks

If a comment shall extend over several lines, then the comment symbol is placed alone on a line:

```
1   body
2     //
3       As many text
4       as you like
```

The following HTML is provided by it:

```
1   <body>
2     <!--
3       As many text
4       as you like
5     -->
6   </body>
```

Caused Comments

Internet Explorer can use sections conditionally, in order to write downwardly compatible HTML code. However, *Pug* has no special syntax. But since every not far recognized text is invariably spent, lines that begin with "<" indications will be transported directly into the HTML.

```
1   <!--[if IE 8]>
2   <html lang="en" class="lt-ie9">
3   <![endif]-->
4   <!--[if gt IE 8]><!-->
5   <html lang="en">
6   <!--<![endif]-->
```

Inherit from Templates

For inheriting templates the keyword "extends" is used. Thus, ranges of the layout page can be overwritten purposefully. First the layout page:

File: layout.pug

```
1   doctype html
2   html
3     head
4       block title
5         title Default title
6     body
7       block content
```

The actual page uses (inherits) this layout page. The range "block" (and therin the range "title") is overwritten. The information is voluntary and, if they are missing, contents of the layout page would be shown.

File: index.pug

```
1   extends layout
2
3   block title
4     title My Articles
5
6   block content
7     h1 Here is some content
```

The final HTML now looks as follows:

```
1   <!doctype html>
2   <html>
3     <head>
4       <title>My Articles</title>
5     </head>
6     <body>
7       <h1>Here is some content</h1>
8     </body>
9   </html>
```

Figure 7-1. *Output of the Master Page*

More Complex Layouts   The inheritance of the layout page can go over several stages, i.e., in a layout page a further can be called. Thus more complex interlocked layouts can be sketched.

Detail for inherting Templates

The simple inheriting of templates can be extended if you specify "block" ranges, which can be overwritten purposefully. A "block" is thereby pug code, which can be replaced. The procedure is recursive.

If the placeholder is equipped with contents, this functions as standard. Regard the following layout page:

File: layout.pug

```
1   html
2     head
3       title My Site - #{title}
4       block scripts
```

```
5            script(src='/jquery.js')
6        body
7          block content
8          block foot
9            #footer
10             p Content of Footer
```

This is now used by means of extends. The page *index.pug* in the following example overwrites thereby the blocks *scripts* and *content*. However, the block *foot* remains unchanged and is taken over by the layout page.

File: index.pug

```
1    extends layout
2
3    block scripts
4      script(src='scripts/jquery.js')
5      script(src='scripts/data.js')
6
7    block content
8      h1= title
9      each pet in pets
10       include pet
```

In a block further blocks can be defined, which are again overwritten with further derivatives of interlocked layout pages. The further layout page *sub-layout.pug* is defined as follows:

File: sub-layout.pug

```
1    extends layout
2
3    block content
4      .sidebar
5        block sidebar
6          p nothing
7      .primary
8        block primary
9          p nothing
```

The page *page-b.pug* now uses this derived layout page:

File: page-b.pug

```
1    extends sub-layout
2
3    block content
4      .sidebar
5        block sidebar
6          p nothing
7      .primary
8        block primary
9          p nothing
```

The blocks *sidebar* and *primary* are overwritten here.

Prepend and append Content Blocks

Apart from blank, replacing contents can also be placed in front (prepend) or supplement (append). With the definition, nothing changes at first:

```
1   html
2     head
3       block head
4         script(src='/vendor/jquery.js')
5         script(src='/vendor/bootstrap.js')
6     body
7       block content
```

Further scripts can now be supplemented as follows:

```
1   extends layout
2
3   block append head
4     script(src='/scripts/data.js')
```

The keyword "block" is optional with the use of "prepend" and "append":

```
1   extends layout
2
3   append head
4     script(src='/scripts/data.js')
```

Q **File Extension**   In this example the file extension *.pug* was omitted. This is optional, if the standard *.pug* is used.

Filter

Filters serve to use another language within the source text. Typical examples are Markdown and CoffeeScript.

```
1   :markdown
2     # Markdown
3
4     I often like including markdown documents.
5
6   script
7     :coffee-script
8       console.log 'This is coffee script'
```

The language block is properly introduced and accordingly interpreted with the ":" indication. The preceding example in HTML looks as follows:

```
1    <h1>Markdown</h1>
2    <p>I often like including markdown documents.</p>
3    <script>console.log('This is coffee script')</script>
```

⚠ **Time of Action**   Filters are implemented by the translation of the page. Within the filter, therefore, no dynamic expressions can stand. The execution for it is very fast.

Partial Pages

Complex pages can be divided—into partial pages, to be exact. Intergration takes place with the keyword includes and the information of the file name, if necessary, with the relative path.

File: index.pug

```
1    doctype html
2    html
3      include ./parts/head.pug
4      body
5        h1 My Site
6        p Welcome to my **super** lame site.
7        include ./includes/foot.pug
```

File: parts/head.pug

```
1    head
2      title Meine Seite
3      script(src='/javascripts/jquery.js')
4      script(src='/javascripts/app.js')
```

File: parts/foot.pug

```
1    #footer
2      p Copyright (c) foobar
```

From this the following HTML develops:

```
1    <!doctype html>
2    <html>
3      <head>
4        <title>My Site</title>
5        <script src='/javascripts/jquery.js'></script>
6        <script src='/javascripts/app.js'></script>
7      </head>
```

```
8     <body>
9       <h1>My Site</h1>
10      <p>Welcome to my super site.</p>
11      <div id="footer">
12        <p>Copyright (c) JoergIsGeek</p>
13      </div>
14    </body>
15  </html>
```

Merge Text

Partial pages do not only have to be *Pug*. Simple text can also be used. *Pug* recognizes this automatically.

index.pug

```
1   doctype html
2   html
3     head
4       style
5         include style.css
6     body
7       h1 My Site
8       p Welcome to my super site.
9       script
10        include script.js
```

style.css

```
1   /* style.css */
2   h1 { color: red; }
```

script.js

```
1   // script.js
2   console.log('You are awesome');
```

From this the following HTML develops:

```
1   <!doctype html>
2   <html>
3     <head>
4       <style>
5         /* style.css */
6         h1 { color: red; }
7       </style>
8     </head>
9     <body>
10      <h1>My Site</h1>
11        <p>Welcome to my super site.</p>
```

```
12        <script>
13          // script.js
14          console.log('You are awesome');
15        </script>
16      </body>
17   </html>
```

Combination of Filters and Partial Pages

With the combination of filters and partial pages, other pages are merged which contain contents in other languages.

File: index.pug

```
1   doctype html
2   html
3     head
4       title An Article
5     body
6       include:markdown article.md
```

The enclosed page is here interpreted as Markdown:

File: article.md

```
1   # Heading in Markdown
2
3   This article has been created in Markdown
```

From this the following HTML develops:

```
1    <!doctype html>
2    <html>
3      <head>
4        <title>An Article</title>
5      </head>
6      <body>
7        <h1>Heading in Markdown</h1>
8        <p>This article has been created in Markdown.</p>
9      </body>
10   </html>
```

The combination with Markdown is especially interesting, because already existing contents can be invariably taken over.

Interpolations

Interpolations replace variables in character sequences. Nearly every programming language probably knows comparable techniques. *Pug* knows the following operators:

- coded character string interpolation

- not coded string interpolation

- Tag Interpolation

Coded Character String Interpolation

In the following template some variables are defined and then used in expressions, without accessing JavaScript syntax again:

```
1   - var title = "Introduction to Node.js";
2   - var author = "Joerg";
3   - var version = "<span>4.1</span>";
4
5   h1= title
6   p Collected by #{author}
7   p #{version}
```

The following HTML shows the result of the interpolation:

```
1   <h1>Introduction to Node.js</h1>
2   <p>Collected by Joerg</p>
3   <p>For Version: &lt;span&gt;4.1!&lt;/span&gt;</p>
```

The code between "#{" and "}" is evaluated, coded and sent as buffered result to the output. The expression can be again JavaScript, so that even more complex expressions can develop.

```
1   - var msg = "really cool";
2   p Dies ist #{msg.toUpperCase()}
```

In this case, rather cool HTML develops from it:

```
1   <p>This is REALLY COOL</p>
```

Not Coded String Interpolation

If security is not necessary or desired in HTML, the not coded variant would work again:

```
1   - var riskyQuote = "<em>Node requires pug.</em>";
2   .quote
3   p Joerg: !{riskyQuote}
```

The HTML is invariably spent:

```
1   <div class="quote">
2       <p>Joerg: <em>Node requires pug.</em></p>
3   </div>
```

Tag Interpolation

Interpolations can also directly be used as tags. For this "#[]" is used.

```
1  p.
2    If you get the sources on #[a(target="_blank", href="https://githu\
3  b.com/pugjs/pug/blob/master/docs/views/reference/interpolation.pug")\
4  GitHub],
5    you'll see, at how many places we use Interpolation.
```

From this quite compact HTML develops:

```
1  <p>If you get the sources on <a target="_blank" href="https://githu\
2  b.com/pugjs/pug/blob/master/docs/views/reference/interpolation.pug">\
3  GitHub</a>,
4    you'll see, at how many places we use Interpolation.
5  </p>
```

The Renderer uses its buffer internally for the tray and for passing on, so that this is better than directly merging HTML.

Mixins (Functions)

Mixins produce re-usable blocks made out of *Pug* code. Thus, endless repetitions of the same HTML components can be avoided. Particularly in connection with Bootstrap, more complex constructs can be prepared and start at any time.

A Mixin (read: Function) is defined as follows:

```
1  mixin list
2    ul
3      li foo
4      li bar
5      li baz
```

The use is based on a special operator:

```
1  +list
2  +list
```

The use is introduced with the "+" indication. In the HTML, nothing more about it can be found:

```
1   <ul>
2     <li>foo</li>
3     <li>bar</li>
4     <li>baz</li>
5   </ul>
6   <ul>
7     <li>foo</li>
8     <li>bar</li>
9     <li>baz</li>
10  </ul>
```

Mixins are JavaScript functions and can be provided with parameters:

```
1   mixin pet(name)
2     li.pet= name
3   ul
4     +pet('Cat')
5     +pet('Dog')
6     +pet('Bird')
```

The following HTML develops from it:

```
1   <ul>
2     <li class="pet">Cat</li>
3     <li class="pet">Dog</li>
4     <li class="pet">Bird</li>
5   </ul>
```

Mixin Blocks

Mixin can take up a block with a *Pug* code and thereby win more dynamics:

```
1    mixin article(title)
2      .article
3        .article-wrapper
4          h1= title
5          if block
6            block
7          else
8            p No Content
9
10   +article('Hello pug')
11
12   +article('Hello pug')
13     p This is an
14     p article about Node.js
```

The following HTML develops from it:

```
1    <div class="article">
2      <div class="article-wrapper">
3        <h1>Hello pug</h1>
4        <p>No content</p>
5      </div>
6    </div>
7    <div class="article">
8      <div class="article-wrapper">
9        <h1>Hello pug</h1>
10       <p>This is an</p>
11       <p>article about Node.js</p>
12     </div>
13   </div>
```

Mixin Attributes

Similar to JavaScript functions, Mixins parameters can take up objects over an implicit "attribute":

```
1   mixin link(href, name)
2     //- attributes == {class: "btn"}
3     a(class!=attributes.class, href=href)= name
4
5   +link('/foo', 'foo')(class="btn")
```

The following HTML develops from it:

```
1   <a href="/foo" class="btn">foo</a>
```

Q The values are coded automatically. If that is not desired, "!=" shall be used. A combination with the "&attributes" is just as possible.

```
1   mixin link(href, name)
2     a(href=href)&attributes(attributes)= name
3
4   +link('/foo', 'foo')(class="btn")
```

The following HTML develops from it:

```
1   <a href="/foo" class="btn">foo</a>
```

Further Arguments

If the number of arguments is only partly variable, a definition of the kind "the whole rest" can be constructed:

```
1   mixin list(id, ...items)
2     ul(id=id)
3       each item in items
4         li= item
5
6   +list('my-list', 1, 2, 3, 4)
```

The following HTML develops from it:

```
1   <ul id="my-list">
2     <li>1</li>
3     <li>2</li>
4     <li>3</li>
5     <li>4</li>
6   </ul>
```

112

Handling Text

Simple text is not interpreted and is not invariably spent, even if it contains control characters.

Connect Text

The "|" operator ("pipe") continues preceding lines simply with text.

```
1  | Simple text can contain <strong>html</strong>
2  p
3      | But it must be alone on the line
```

The text arrives invariably in the HTML page:

```
1  Simple text can contain <strong>html</strong>
2  <p>But it must be alone on the line</p>
```

Inline in Tag

Tags in Tags are at the agenda in HTML. Because in nearly each block element are various inline elements to find (<span> in <div>). Text after an element is invariably taken over and can contain HTML. That is often simpler to define than the complete hierarchy:

```
1  p Simple text can contain <strong>HTML</strong>
```

The HTML arrives invariably in the page:

```
1  <p>Simple text can contain <strong>HTML</strong> </p>
```

Block in Tag

Often large blocks with text are needed. Scripts or longer style definitions are good examples of it. Here interactivity is required rarely. In order to introduce such a block, the element instruction point becomes a "." placed behind itself:

```
1  script.
2    if (usingpug)
3      console.log('you are awesome')
4    else
5      console.log('use pug')
```

The contents arrive invariably in the page:

```
1  <script>
2    if (usingpug)
3      console.log('you are awesome')
4    else
5      console.log('use pug')
6  </script>
```

Handling Tags

Tags are only described by their name, without the Markup clips.
The hierarchy is specified by the indentation (two blanks).

```
1   ul
2     li Item A
3     li Item B
4     li Item C
```

From this example valid HTML develops:

```
1   <ul>
2     <li>Item A</li>
3     <li>Item B</li>
4     <li>Item C</li>
5   </ul>
```

If the Doctype requires this, self-closing elements will be produced automatically. For the element "img", this looks as follows:

```
1   img
```

Here valid HTML develops with a closing tag:

```
1   <img/>
```

Extension of Blocks

Interlocked blocks can be defined in a line, as long as no contents follow. This takes place via ":" operator. This takes place with frequent typical combinations, for example with hyperlinks:

```
1   a: img
```

From this example valid HTML develops as follows:

```
1   <a><img/></a>
```

Self-Closing Tags

Some tags, such as img, meta, and link never contain contents.
They are therefore self-closing, except with the XML Doctype. If this is to be shown independently of the Doctype, this can take place with concluding "/" indications.

```
1   meta/
2   link(rel='stylesheet')/
```

From this example the following HTML develops:

```
1   <meta/>
2   <link rel="stylesheet"/>
```

CHAPTER 8

The Pug Command Line

The command line can use auxiliary functions directly, for example translating sites into static HTML at first.

Installing the Command Line

The installation takes place via **npm** (*-g* stands for global).

```
1    $ npm install pug -g
```

 CLI Command line tools are often called "CLI": Command Line Interface.

Use and Options

The use of the command line looks as follows:

```
1    $ pug [options] [dir|file ...]
```

Table 8-1. *Options of Pug-CLI*

Options	
-h, --help	help for usage
-V, --version	version of the library
-O, --obj <path|str>	JavaScript options or JSON file with a suitable object inside
-o, --out <dir>	edition listing for the HTML
-p, --path <path>	file path for dissolving ' includes '
-P, --pretty	HTML edition is arranged readable
-c, --client	translation functions for the client page *runtime.js*

(continued)

© Jörg Krause 2017

J. Krause, *Programming Web Applications with Node, Express and Pug*, DOI 10.1007/978-1-4842-2511-0_8

Table 8-1. (*continued*)

Options	
-n, --name <str>	the name of the translated template (requires – client)
-D, --no-debug	translate without debuggers (smaller functions)
-w, --watch	supervises files on changes and renders again
-E, --extension <ext>	indicates the file extension for the edition
--name-after-file	name of the template after the last segment of the file path during (requires – client, overwritten by –name)
--doctype <str>	determines the doctype on the command line (meaningful, if the template)

Sample Applications for the Command Line

Translate templates locally as follows:

1   `$ pug templates`

To produce two HTML files, "foo.html" and "bar.html", thew following command will work:

1   `$ pug {foo,bar}.pug`

Pug results can be shown via "stdio":

1   `$ pug <my.pug> my.html`

A bypass to *Pug* takes place via the pipe symbol:

1   `$ echo "h1 pug!" | pug`

Render the listings "foo" and "bar" after */tmp*:

1   `$ pug foo bar --out /tmp`

Appendix

Configuration of the file package.json

This section summarizes all features for the configuration of the file *package.json*.

Meaning of the Configuration Elements

The features can have various effects. It is recommended to argue with some of it at the beginning precisely. The configuration of the package, thus the execution of **npm config**, influences the available features.

Some features are only relevant if the application is to be published as a new package on NPM. This does not apply in most cases. You can then ignore the appropriate options.

Name

Name and version are the most important fields. The name is required. From names and version, a clear ID of the package is created. It is assumed that your application becomes again installable as package. That is practical and meaningful, but not necessarily needed. For the name, there are some rules due to the coupling to the package manager:

- The name may have a maximum of 214 characters.

- The name should not start with a dot or underline.

- Capital letters are not allowed.

- The name is used both on the command line and as part of a URL, thus the name choice must correspond to the conditions predominating in these envrionments.

In addition, you should absolutely avoid collisions with existing packages. Name components like "node" or "js" are not a good idea. That this is about JavaScript "js" should be clear.

version

If packages are published, the version is enormously important. Each package will develop further and then a distinction must be met. The package **node-semver** must be able to process the version number. (We'll come back to this later on.)

© Jörg Krause 2017
J. Krause, *Programming Web Applications with Node, Express and Pug*, DOI 10.1007/978-1-4842-2511-0

description

The field description is helpful to indicate a meaningful description.

keywords

Keywords serve to find packages in the Repository. If you do not publish your package, you can omit the field.

homepage

If a homepage exists, indicate the URL here. Do not confuse this feature with "URL".

bugs

Here an URL is entered to a Bugtracking Application. This is an object with two further features.

```
1  {
2    url" : "https://github.com/joergisageek/nodejs-samples",
3    "email" : "bugs@joergkrause.de"
4  }
```

license

For published packages. you have the option here of indicating the license. You find practical proposals under the following URL:

- *http://opensource.org/licenses*

The current usual information corresponds to SPDX expressions, for example:

```
{ "license": "(MIT OR Apache-2.0)" }
```

If the package will not be published no matter what, set the feature private to true.

However, if you publish it, then you call the author (in each case only one) and employee (an array of people).

files

This is an array of files, which are part of the package. You can indicate a folder here, the contents of which are then completely loaded. However, there are further rules which can exclude elements from the folder. For example, it is possible to indicate a file as the name *.npmignore* (in the root of the project), in which files are listed, which will not become part of this package.

main

This is the module ID, which serves as entry point in this application. If the package is used as part of another application, the developer of this application can request the use as follows:

```
require('Modul-ID')
```

In this instance, the script is called which was indicated in `main`. Normally, only the `exports` object should be here, thus the publicly available elements. The information of a script is relative to the master folder.

bin

Here executable files are indicated, which are made available in the path ('PATH') of the operating system. With `bin`, a list of commands is agreed upon, which have executable instructions assigned. **npm** will now create a link on *prefix/bin* with global commands. With local instructions the path becomes *./node_modules/.bin/*. An example looks as follows:

```
1  {
2    "bin" : {
3    "myapp" : "./cli.js"
4    }
5  }
```

The script *cli.js* is executed via the command */usr/local/bin/myapp*.

 Linux and Windows   This functions in the form shown not only for Unix operating systems. For Windows, **npm** creates a Wrapper on the command line **cmd**, over which Node is called. In addition, the script with the line `#!/usr/bin/envnode` must be introduced. Windows ignores this, but the Wrapper reacts to it.

---

directories

With this feature, the structure of the package can be defined. Most values are more or less freely usable; it concerns more meta data.

- *lib*: The mass of the components of a library.
- *Bin*: Elements in this folder are treated as child elements of the `bin` path, if there is nothing.
- *man*: The list of the instructions (`man` pages).
- *Doc*: Documentations in Markdown.
- *example*: Examples.

repository

The place where the code lies. This is important for other developers who participate in the development.

```
1  "repository" : {
2    "type" : "git",
3    "url" : "https://github.com/npm/npm.git"
4  }
5
```

```
6   "repository" : {
7       "type" : "svn",
8       "url" : "https://v8.googlecode.com/svn/trunk/"
9   }
```

The URL should be public for everything/everyone involved. The Repository may, however, be written in a protected way. Version control systems should be able to process the indicated URL directly. Remember not to refer to a HTML page here. This information is for a machine, not for humans.

Some important public Repositories have short forms:

- "repository": "npm/npm"

- "repository": "gist:11081aaa281"

- "repository": "bitbucket:example/repo"

- "repository": "gitlab:another/repo"

scripts

Each package has a certain lifetime with different phases. This feature specifies which scripts are to be processed with which phases. Phases are, for example, "start" or "test":

```
1   {
2       "name": "death-clock",
3       "version": "1.0.0",
4       "scripts": {
5           "start": "node server.js",
6           "test": "mocha --reporter spec test"
7       },
8       "devDependencies": {
9           "mocha": "^1.17.1"
10      }
11  }
```

config

The configuration object illustrates user specific settings. The information covers standard settings.

```
1   {
2       "name" : "mein-paket",
3       "config" : {
4           "port" : "8080"
5       }
6   }
```

The user of the package can provide this at the installation with changes of these settings. In the package itself, the configuration object is globally available. Changes take place with **npm**:

```
npm config set mein-paket:port 8001
```

dependencies

Dependence is defined by means of names and version numbers. Packages can exist locally or load from Git.

⚲ Developer Packages   Packages, which specifically support the development process, should not be indicated here. This concerns, for example, Transpiler or test environments. For these the parameter "devDependencies" is responsible.

For the version number, there is a special semantic:

- `version`: The version must be accurately exact.

- `&gt;version`: Version must be larger than the information.

- `&gt;=version`: Version must be larger or equal to the information.

- `&lt;version`: Version must be smaller than the information.

- `&lt;=version`: : Version must be smaller or equal to the information.

- `~version`: Main and underversion must fit.

- `^version`: : Version must be compatible.

- `* or ""`: Every version.

- `version1 - version2`: Corresponds >=version1 <=version2.

- `area1 || ares2` Either area1 or area2/

- `Url or Pfad`

All the following are valid references:

```
1   { "dependencies" :
2     { "foo" : "1.0.0 - 2.9999.9999"
3     , "bar" : ">=1.0.2 <2.1.2"
4     , "baz" : ">1.0.2 <=2.3.4"
5     , "boo" : "2.0.1"
6     , "qux" : "<1.0.0 || >=2.3.1 <2.4.5 || >=2.5.2 <3.0.0"
7     , "asd" : "http://asdf.com/asdf.tar.gz"
8     , "til" : "~1.2"
9     , "elf" : "~1.2.3"
10    , "two" : "2.x"
11    , "thr" : "3.3.x"
12    , "lat" : "latest"
13    , "dyl" : "file:../dyl"
14    }
15  }
```

If an URL is indicated, a compressed package (Tarball) can hide itself behind it. If this is the case, the package will be loaded and installed locally to the application without a second thought. As source, a Repository of a Git server, in particular Github, works, too. URLs which refer to Git can have the following formats:

```
1  git://github.com/user/project.git#commit-ish
2  git+ssh://user@hostname:project.git#commit-ish
3  git+ssh://user@hostname/project.git#commit-ish
4  git+http://user@hostname/project/blah.git#commit-ish
5  git+https://user@hostname/project/blah.git#commit-ish
```

The information for the placeholder *commit-ish* can be the tag (brand), SHA fingerprint (Hash) or the name of a branch. If nothing is indicated, the value is master.

If the format "user/project" is used, automatic access to Github takes place.

```
1  {
2    "name": "foo",
3    "version": "0.0.0",
4    "dependencies": {
5      "express": "visionmedia/express",
6      "mocha": "visionmedia/mocha#4727d357ea"
7    }
8  }
```

Local paths are addressed by the Moniker "file". If npm install –save is used, the data local to the project will be stored:

```
1  ../foo/bar
2  ~/foo/bar
3  ./foo/bar
4  /foo/bar
```

If you use **npm**, then the paths are always normalized as soon as you're entering something into the file *package.json* and indicating relatively:

```
1  {
2    "name": "baz",
3    "dependencies": {
4      "bar": "file:../foo/bar"
5    }
6  }
```

The information of local paths can be meaningful for developments, if the access is also supposed to be possible offline. However, if packages are published later, you should absolutely avoid local paths.

devDependencies

With this information all dependence will be defined, which is needed for the development period. Otherwise you behave as described in "dependencies".

```
1   { "name": "coffee-project",
2       "description": "Ein Projekt, dass Coffee-Script benutzt",
3       "version": "1.2.3",
4       "devDependencies": {
5           "coffee-script": "~1.6.3"
6       },
7       "scripts": {
8           "prepublish": "coffee -o lib/ -c src/book.coffee"
9       },
10      "main": "lib/server.js"
11  }
```

Here the Transpiler "Coffeescript" is used. When publishing, the Transpiler will be used, to translate the CoffeeScript files into JavaScript, and then deliver the finished files.

peerDependencies

In some cases, compatibility with a tool or library is guaranteed without this tool or library being used. Thus it is shown that a use can be possible.

```
1   {
2     "name": "book-sample",
3     "version": "1.3.5",
4     "peerDependencies": {
5       "book-node": "2.x"
6     }
7   }
```

This information shows that the package "book-sample" is compatible with the version 2.x of the package "*book-node*". The command npm install book-sample will dissolve the following dependence, if a version 2.3.0 from "book-node" exists:

```
1   ├────── book-sample@1.3.5
2   └────── book-node@2.3.0
```

The use of this setting serves the configuration of Plugins. Here the Plugin depends on its "*host*", however, it does not need this explicitly in order to be installed.

bundledDependencies

Dependence in this section is distributed if you publish a part of the package along with it.

optionalDependencies

Optional dependence is dissolved and treated like regular if the packages are found. However, if **npm** cannot dissolve a name, an error is normally produced. With optional dependence **npm** will simply continue if the dissolution fails.

The program itself must naturally react to missing packages, otherwise errors will occur during run time. This can look as follows:`

```
1   try {
2     var foo = require('foo')
3     var fooVersion = require('foo/package.json').version
4   } catch (er) {
5     foo = null
6   }
7   if (checkVersion(fooVersion) ) {
8     foo = null
9   }
10
11  // In the program:
12
13  if (foo) {
14    foo.doFooThings()
15  }
```

Here the instruction "require" failed because an optional package was not loaded. The private method 'checkVersion' is used in order to examine the package if it was not loaded for the correct version. Functionality supplied by a package is called only if the package was loaded and the correct version is present.

engines

With this information a certain version of Node itself is determined:

```
1   {
2     "engines" : {
3       "node" : ">=0.10.3 <0.12"
4     }
5   }
```

ℹ   Don't confuse the information with the term "Engine", which is also used for a Webframework such as "Express".

Aside from Node, the version of **npm** can also be determined:

```
1   {
2     "engines" : {
3       "npm" : "~1.0.20"
4     }
5   }
```

124

os

Some functions of Node can be dependent on the operating system. They can therefore determine on which operating system the package can be used:

```
"os" : [ "darwin", "linux" ]
```

It is often simpler to exclude a not-supported operating system and thus permit all different:

```
"os" : [ "!win32" ]
```

In Node itself this serves the call of "process.platform", which helps to determine the operating system.

cpu

With this information the processor architecture is determined.

```
"cpu" : [ "x64", "ia32" ]
```

Also, here individual architectures can be excluded:

```
"cpu" : [ "!arm", "!mips" ]
```

Node supplies the actual value at the run time of 'process.arch'.

preferGlobal

If the package is a tool, a command line, or global script, then this is useful to show the information. It is possible to install the package locally nevertheless; however, you'll then see a warning. The value is boolean ("true" or "false").

private

Private packages, which are not intended to be published, are marked as private. The value is boolean (true or false). This prevents inadvertent publishing to a Repository.

publishConfig

The accommodated values here are used at the time of publication. That concerns all features, especially features such as tag and registry. Thus it can be prevented that a package gets the value latest automatically, although it concerns the path of an earlier version.

The Default Values

npm uses some default values, if the appropriate information is missing.

```
"scripts": {"start": "node server.js"}
```

If the file *server.js* exists, it is assumed that it is the starting file.

```
"scripts":{"preinstall": "node-gyp rebuild"}
```

If a file with the name *binding.gyp* exists, 'node-gyp' will be used.

 Gyp   '*node-gyp*' is a command line tool, which translates native extensions for Node. It serves to make native packages available platform-independently. The tool worries about the features of different platforms. In addition, see:

https://github.com/nodejs/node-gyp.

```
"contributors": [...]
```

If a file *AUTHORS* exists, each line is used as an entry in the array. The format of each line is thereby Name '<email>' (url). Lines with a "#" or blank at the beginning are ignored.

Brief description
Reference Node.js Modules

The brief description summarizes all integrated Node functions clearly.

HTTP

```
var http = require('http');
```

The simplest Web server at a glance:

```
1   http.createServer(function (request, response) {
2     response.writeHead(200, {'Content-Type': 'text/plain'});
3     response.end('Hello World\n');
4   }).listen(8124);
5
6   console.log('Server running at http://127.0.0.1:8124/');
```

http.STATUS_CODES;

> All status codes and a short description in addition.

http.request(options, [callback]);

> Function for sending requirements.

http.get(options, [callback]);

> A complete "GET" requirement including the "end" call

Server

server = http.createServer([requestListener]);

> Provides a new Web server object. The callback function *requestListener* receives the request.

server.listen(port, [hostname], [backlog], [callback]);

> Start of the receiving of messages with Host and Port.

server.listen(path, [callback]);

> Start of the receiving of messages with UNIX Socket and path.

server.listen(handle, [callback]);

> Start of the receiving of messages with Handle (server or Socket).

server.close([callback]);

> Terminates the receiving of messages.

server.setTimeout(msecs, callback);

> The maximum time which is waited for a connection.

server.maxHeadersCount;

> The maximum number of head fields, which are accepted. 1000 are the standard, 0 stand for unlimited.

server.timeout;

> The maximum time which is waited for a connection. Setting takes place with "setTimeout".

server.on('request', function (request, response) { });

> Event which fires with each requirement (request).

server.on('connection', function (socket) { });

> Event fire, if new TCP Stream was provided.

server.on('close', function () { });

> Event fires if the connection was closed.

server.on('checkContinue', function (request, response) { });

> Event fires if *Expect: 100-continue* was recognized.

server.on('connect', function (request, socket, head) { });

> Event which fires with each connecting attempt (HTTP-CONNECT).

server.on('upgrade', function (request, socket, head) { });

> Event which fires with every Upgrade, from HTTP 1.1 to 2.0 or WebSockets.

server.on('clientError', function (exception, socket) { });

> Event which fires with each error condition of the client.

Request

request.write(chunk, [encoding]);

>   Sends a part data.

request.end([data], [encoding]);

>   Terminates sending the data; data not yet sent is now transferred.

request.abort();

>   A requirement cancels.

request.setTimeout(timeout, [callback]);

>   Sets the time delimitation for the underlying Socket sets.

request.setNoDelay([noDelay]);

>   Turns the Nagle algorithm off. This serves with TCP for buffering data before sending.

request.setSocketKeepAlive([enable], [initialDelay]);

>   Keeps the connection open.

request.on('response', function(response) { });

>   Event fires if an answer was received.

request.on('socket', function(socket) { });

>   Event fires if a Socket was assigned.

request.on('connect', function(response, socket, head) { });

>   Event fires if a server answers a request with CONNECT. If this is not treated, the connection is closed again.

request.on('upgrade', function(response, socket, head) { });

>   Event fires if the server answers an upgrade request.

request.on('continue', function() { });

>   Event fires, if the server sends *100 Continue* (usually as reaction to a *Expect: 100-continue* request).

Response

response.write(chunk, [encoding]);

>   Sends a part of the answer. Head fields are sent before, if this did not take place with 'writeHead' before it.

response.writeContinue();

>   Sends HTTP/1.1 100 Continue.

response.writeHead(statusCode, [reasonPhrase], [headers]);

>   Sends the head fields.

response.setTimeout(msecs, callback);

> Specify the maximum of exceeding time.

response.setHeader(name, value);

> Provides a head field. An already available one with the same name will be replaced. If several identical head fields are needed, an array can be used.

response.getHeader(name);

> Determines a head field, which was made available but not sent yet.

response.removeHeader(name);

> Removes a head field, which was made available, however, not sent yet.

response.addTrailers(headers);

> Inserts the HTTP Trailing head field.

response.end([data], [encoding]);

> Signalizes that all head fields and data were sent. Must be used.

response.statusCode;

> Status code, which is sent if the head fields are implicitly sent.
>
> With explicit sending with 'writeHead', the code is used by this method.

response.headersSent;

> Shows "true", if the head fields were sent.

response.sendDate;

> If "true", the date head field *Date* will be automatically produced.

response.on('close', function () { });

> Event fires if the connection before the use of "end" is closed.

response.on('finish', function() { });

> Event fires if the answer was sent.

Message

message.httpVersion;

> The version of protocol HTTP.

message.headers;

> An object with head fields.

message.trailers;

> Trailer after "end" (when sending in blocks).

message.method;

> The method (or verb), thus GET, POST, etc.

message.url;

> The URL.

message.statusCode;

> The status code (100, 200, 404 etc.)

message.socket;

> The underlying Socket object.

message.setTimeout(msecs, callback);

> Determines the time limit of the connection.

Global

__filename;

> Name of the implemented file as absolute path.

__dirname;

> Name of the current folder.

module;

> Reference to the current module. module.exports makes the data available, which can be requested with require.

exports;

> An abbreviation for module.exports.

process;

> The process under which the current script is implemented.

Buffer;

> The class with which handling binary data takes place.

Console

console.log([data], [...]);

> Output on standard output with radical change.

console.info([data], [...]);

> Output on standard output with radical change.

console.error([data], [...]);

> Output on error output with radical change.

console.warn([data], [...]);

> Output on error output with radical change.

console.dir(obj);

> Uses util.inspect for a formatted output of objects.

console.time(label);

> Starts time measurement.

console.timeEnd(label);

> Terminates time measurement.

console.trace(label);

> Shows the Stacktrace.

console.assert(expression, [message]);

> Tests an expression and gives the AssertionError, if the expression is 'false'.

Timer

setTimeout(callback, delay, [arg], [...]);

> Delays the unique execution of a callback function.

clearTimeout(t);

> Stops the execution.

setInterval(callback, delay, [arg], [...]);

> Delays the repeated execution of a callback function.

clearInterval(t);

> Stops the execution of the intervals.

setImmediate(callback, [arg], [...]);

> A more highly prioritized callback function.

clearImmediate(immediateObject);

> Stops the execution.

unref();

> Interval timer, which is implemented only for as long as Node runs.

ref();

> Interval times, which is only as long implemented as Node is open.

Module

Modules can be floated from a file:

```
1   var module = require('./module.js');
```

> You load a module as follows if require was requested in this module:1
> module.require('./another_module.js');

module.id;

> The ID of the module; normally this is the file name.

module.filename;

> The file name of the module.

module.loaded;

> Condition of the loading procedure; becomes true if the module is completely loaded.

module.parent;

> The module that the current module requested.

module.children;

> The modules which were requested.

One direct way public interfaces can be made available:

```
1   exports.area = function (r) {
2       return 3.14 * r * r;
3   };
```

However, if a constructor or a complex object with several features is to be exported, use the following syntax:

```
1   module.exports = function(width) {
2       return {
3         area: function() {
4             return width * width;
5         }
6       };
7   }
```

Process

process.on('exit', function(code) {});

> Event fires if a process ends.

process.on('uncaughtException', function(err) {});

> Event fires if an exception did not become finished (imprisoned).

`process.stdout;`

> A writable stream to the standard output.

`process.stderr;`

> A writable stream to the error output.

`process.stdin;`

> A readable stream to the standard input.

`process.argv;`

> The arguments of the command line.

`process.env;`

> The user environment of the console.

`process.execPath;`

> Path of the executable file of the process.

`process.execArgv;`

> Node-specified command line options.

`process.arch;`

> The processor architecture ('arm', 'ia32' or 'x64').

`process.config;`

> An JSON object which contains the options, with which Node was compiled.

`process.pid;`

> PID of the processor.

`process.platform;`

> The platform, e.g. 'darwin', 'freebsd', 'linux', 'sunos' or 'win32'.

`process.title;`

> Name of the process with expenditures, writable.

`process.version;`

> Output of NODE_VERSION.

`process.versions;`

> Versions of Node and dependent modules.

`process.abort();`

> Terminates Node and produces a Dump.

`process.chdir(dir);`

> Changes the work listing for Node.

`process.cwd();`

> Changes the work listing for the process.

`process.exit([code]);`

> Terminates the process.

`process.getgid();`

> Reads the ID of the process group.

`process.setgid(id);`

> Writes the ID of the process group.

`process.getuid();`

> Reads the ID of the identity, under which the process runs.

`process.setuid(id);`

> Writes the ID of the identity, under which the process runs.

`process.getgroups();`

> Reads the group IDs of the process group.

`process.setgroups(grps);`

> Writes the group IDs of the process group.

`process.initgroups(user, extra_grp);`

> Reads and initializes the access list for groups.

`process.kill(pid, [signal]);`

> Sends "kill" to the process.

`process.memoryUsage();`

> Determines an object, which describes the condition of the memory.

`process.nextTick(callback);`

> Call of the callback function *callback* with the next spleen of the event loop.

`process.umask([mask]);`

> Writes or reads the rights of the process.

`process.uptime();`

> The amount of time Node has been running.

`process.hrtime();`

> A highly soluble array "[seconds, nanoseconds]" of material time.

ChildProcess

ChildProcess;

> Class for the treatment of subprocesses.

child.stdin;

> A writable stream to the standard input.

child.stdout;

> A readable stream to the standard output.

child.stderr;

> A readable stream to the error output.

child.pid;

> PID of the process.

child.connected;

> Is "true" if the under process can receive messages.

child.kill([signal]);

> Terminates the process.

child.send(message, [sendHandle]);

> Sends a message.

child.disconnect();

> Terminates the connection of the subprocess.

child_process.spawn(command, [args], [options]);

> Starts a new process with arguments.

child_process.exec(command, [options], callback);

> Starts a new process in a command line (Shell).

child_process.execFile(file, [args], [options], [callback]);

> Starts a new process by the call of an executable file in a command line (Shell).

child_process.fork(modulePath, [args], [options]);

> Like "spawn", but with a communication channel.

Util

util.format(format, [...]);

> Formatted output, like printf (%s, %d, %j).

util.debug(string);

> Synchronous output to the error output with buffer.

util.error([...]);

> Synchronous output to the error output without buffers.

util.puts([...]);

> Synchronous output to the standard output with a line break after each argument.

util.print([...]);

> Synchronous output to the standard output without line break after each argument.

util.log(string);

> Output with timestamp to the standard output.

util.inspect(object, [opts]);

> Character string representation of objects. *opts* can contain "showHidden", "depth", "colors" and "customInspect".

util.isArray(object);

> It checks if an object is an array.

util.isRegExp(object);

> It checks if an object is a regular expression (in object form, 'RegExp').

util.isDate(object);

> It checks if an object is date (in object form, 'Date').

util.isError(object);

> It checks if an object is an error object ('Error').

util.inherits(constructor, superConstructor);

> Inherits prototypical methods from a constructor to another.

Events

emitter.addListener(event, listener);

> Adds an event and the suitable event working methods.

emitter.on(event, listener);

> Adds an event and the suitable event working method. Short form for comfortable use.

emitter.once(event, listener);

> Adds an event and the suitable event working method. The method is only called once.

emitter.removeListener(event, listener);

> Removes the event working method from an event.

`emitter.removeAllListeners([event]);`

> Removes all event working methods from an event.

`emitter.setMaxListeners(n);`

> Specifies the maximum number of event working methods. According to standard, a warning is produced at 10.

`emitter.listeners(event);`

> Returns all event working methods as array.

`emitter.emit(event, [arg1], [arg2], [...]);`

> Implements all event working methods with the arguments.

`EventEmitter.listenerCount(emitter,    event);`

> Determines the number of event working methods.

Stream

Streams can be writable or readable or both. That depends on where they come from. "readable" stands in the following for readable ones, "writable", however, for writable ones.

`readable.on('readable', function() {});`

> Fires the event if the data is readable.

`readable.on('data', function(chunk) {});`

> If data arrives block-by-block, this event fires if a data block arrives.

`readable.on('end', function() {});`

> If data arrives block-by-block, this event fires if no more data is present.

`readable.on('close', function() {});`

> Fires the event, if the connection was closed.

`readable.on('error', function() {});`

> Fires the event if an error arose.

`readable.read([size]);`

> Reads a number of bytes.

`readable.setEncoding(encoding);`

> Sets the coding if a character string is used.

`readable.resume();`

> Continues the sending of events.

`readable.pause();`

> Stops the sending of events.

`readable.pipe(destination, [options]);`

> Reads all data and writes them to the goal.

`readable.unpipe([destination]);`

Terminates the connection between source and a goal, which was developed by the means of "pipe".

`readable.unshift(chunk);`

Returns data which is not needed, but was already read by the optimizations.

`writable.write(chunk, [encoding], [callback]);`

Writes a data block in the stream and calls the callback function, as soon as this is terminated.

`writer.once('drain', write);`

An event that uniquely fires if data was written and stream is ready to assume more data.

`writable.end([chunk], [encoding], [callback]);`

It shows that the letter is terminated.

`writer.on('finish', function() {});`

An event fires if after the end of the transmission, all data is handed over to the operating system with "end".

`writer.on('pipe', function(src) {});`

An event fires if on a readable stream, a further writable data sink was added.

`writer.on('unpipe', function(src) {});`

An event that fires if a writable data sink was removed on a readable stream.

`writer.on('error', function(src) {});`

An event that fires if an error arose.

File System

In many methods, there is a synchronous (Sync) and asynchronous (without marking) version. Asynchronous ones return data over the callback function; synchronous return a value. With asynchronous functioning errors are returned as exception object as the first argument of the callback function; with synchronous functioning the exceptions are released. Variants with the argument *fd* use a file description (file descriptor) instead of the file name.

- `fs.rename(oldPath, newPath, callback);`
- **`fs.renameSync(oldPath, newPath);`**

Designates a file.

- `fs.ftruncate(fd, len, callback);`
- `fs.ftruncateSync(fd, len);`
- `fs.truncate(path, len, callback);`
- **`fs.truncateSync(path, len);`**

Cuts a file off at the position.

- `fs.chown(path, uid, gid, callback);`
- `fs.chownSync(path, uid, gid);`
- `fs.fchown(fd, uid, gid, callback);`
- `fs.fchownSync(fd, uid, gid);`
- `fs.lchown(path, uid, gid, callback);`
- **`fs.lchownSync(path, uid, gid);`**

Changes the owner of a file.

- `fs.chmod(path, mode, callback);`
- `fs.chmodSync(path, mode);`
- `fs.fchmod(fd, mode, callback);`
- `fs.fchmodSync(fd, mode);`
- `fs.lchmod(path, mode, callback);`
- **`fs.lchmodSync(path, mode);`**

Changes the access rights to a file.

- `fs.stat(path, callback);`
- `fs.statSync(path);`
- `fs.lstat(path, callback);`
- `fs.lstatSync(path);`
- `fs.fstat(fd, callback);`
- **`fs.fstatSync(fd);`**

Returns rights to a file. That prefix 'l' shows that symbolic links are accessed.

- `fs.link(srcpath, dstpath, callback);`
- `fs.linkSync(srcpath, dstpath);`
- **`fs.symlinkSync(srcpath, dstpath, [type]);`**

Creates a link (hard link) and/or symbolic link (soft link).

- `fs.readlink(path, callback);`
- **`fs.readlinkSync(path);`**

Reads a link (not the file behind it).

- `fs.unlink(path, callback);`
- **`fs.unlinkSync(path);`**

Delets a link and/or a file, if the paths points directly to a file.

- fs.realpath(path, [cache], callback);
- **fs.realpathSync(path, [cache]);**

Determines the complete, absolute path.

- fs.rmdir(path, callback);
- **fs.rmdirSync(path);**

Removes a folder.

- fs.mkdir(path, [mode], callback);
- **fs.mkdirSync(path, [mode]);**

Provides a folder. The standard mode is 0777 (all rights).

- fs.readdir(path, callback);
- **fs.readdirSync(path);**

Reads the contents of a folder and returns the file list.

- fs.close(fd, callback);
- fs.closeSync(fd);

Closes a file.

- fs.open(path, flags, [mode], callback);
- **fs.openSync(path, flags, [mode]);**

Opens a file for reading and writing operations.

- fs.utimes(path, atime, mtime, callback);
- fs.utimesSync(path, atime, mtime);
- fs.futimes(fd, atime, mtime, callback);
- **fs.futimesSync(fd, atime, mtime);**

Changes the file date.

- fs.fsync(fd, callback);
- **fs.fsyncSync(fd);**

Synchronizes the condition of the file with the data storage unit.

- fs.write(fd, buffer, offset, length, position, callback);
- fs.writeSync(fd, buffer, offset, length, position);
- fs.writeFile(filename, data, [options], callback);
- **fs.writeFileSync(filename, data, [options]);**

Writes data into a file.

- fs.read(fd, buffer, offset, length, position, callback);
- fs.readSync(fd, buffer, offset, length, position);
- fs.readFile(filename, [options], callback);
- **fs.readFileSync(filename, [options]);**

Reads from a file byte by byte into a buffer. If a coding like 'utf8' is configured in the settings, the data will be read as character string.

- fs.appendFile(filename, data, [options], callback);
- **fs.appendFileSync(filename, data, [options]);**

Hangs data at the end of an existing file.

- **fs.watch(filename, [options], [listener]);**

Supervises changes on a file and releases the callback function *listener* when something is changed.

- fs.exists(path, callback);
- **fs.existsSync(path);**

It checks if a file exists.

The stat function returns a Stats object, which has the following methods:

- stats.isFile()
- stats.isDirectory()
- stats.isBlockDevice()
- stats.isCharacterDevice()
- stats.isSymbolicLink()
- stats.isFIFO()
- stats.isSocket()

fs.createReadStream(path, [options]);

> Produces an object of the type 'ReadStream'.

fs.createWriteStream(path, [options]);

> Produces an object of the type 'WriteStream'.

Path

path.normalize(p);

> Normalizes a path with consideration from '..' and '.'.

path.join([path1], [path2], [...]);

> Connects parts to a valid path.

path.resolve([from ...], to);

> Dissolution to an absolute path.

`path.relative(from, to);`

> Dissolution of a relative path.

`path.dirname(p);`

> Name of the folder.

`path.basename(p, [ext]);`

> Last part of a path.

`path.extname(p);`

> The file extension.

`path.sep;`

> The platform-specific separator for files, '\' or '/'.

`path.delimiter;`

> The platform-specific separator for paths, ';' or ':'.

URL

`url.parse(url, [parseQuerystring], [slashesDenoteHost]);`

> Transfers a URL as character string into an object.

`url.format(urlObj);`

> Transfers an object in a URL.

`url.resolve(from, to);`

> Simulate the URL production as the Anchor Tag in HTML would do.

Querystring

`querystring.stringify(obj, [sep], [eq]);`

> Provides a Querystring from an object.

`querystring.parse(str, [sep], [eq], [options]);`

> Provides an object from a Querystring.

Assert

`assert.fail(actual, expected, message, operator);`

> Throws an exception.

`assert(value, message);`
`assert.ok(value, [message]);`

> Tests, if a value is true.

`assert.equal(actual, expected, [message]);`

> Tests values on equality. Objects become only flat – on the first level – compared.

`assert.notEqual(actual, expected, [message]);`

> Tests values on inequality. Objects become only flat – on the first level – compared.

`assert.deepEqual(actual, expected, [message]);`

> Tests values on equality. Objects become deep – on all levels – compared.

`assert.notDeepEqual(actual, expected, [message]);`

> Tests values on inequality. Objects become deep – on all levels – compared.

`assert.strictEqual(actual, expected, [message]);`

> Tests values on equality with '===' - the operator.

`assert.notStrictEqual(actual, expected, [message]);`

> Tests values on inequality with '!==' - operator.

`assert.throws(block, [error], [message]);`

> Expects that the code block throws an exception.

`assert.doesNotThrow(block, [message]);`

> Expects that the code block throws no exception.

`assert.ifError(value);`

> Checks if the value is "false".

OS

`os.tmpdir();`

> Standard listing for temporary files.

`os.endianness();`

> Type of CPU; "LE" or "BE" – low endian or big endian.

`os.hostname();`

> The name of the host.

`os.type();`

> The name of the operating system.

`os.platform();`

> The name of the platform.

`os.arch();`

> Architecture of the CPU (x86, x64, ARM, etc.).

os.release();

>   Version of the operating system.

os.uptime();

>   Amount of time the system has been running for.

os.loadavg();

>   Middle load times.

s.totalmem();

>   Memory

os.freemem();

>   Free memory

os.cpus();

>   Array of objects, whereby each entry stands for a CPU/ a core.

os.networkInterfaces();

>   List of network interfaces.

os.EOL;

>   Line end character for this operating system.

Buffer

new   Buffer(size);

>   Provides a new buffer with the indicated size.

new   Buffer(array);

>   Provides a new buffer with the indicated size of the array.

new   Buffer(str,   [encoding]);

>   Provides a new buffer for character strings with the indicated coding.

Buffer.isEncoding(encoding);

>   Checks if the coding ('utf8', etc.) is valid.

Buffer.isBuffer(obj);

>   Tests, if an object is a "buffer".

Buffer.concat(list,   [totalLength]);

>   Joins Buffer.

Buffer.byteLength(string, [encoding]);

>   Length of a character string in bytes (depends on the coding).

`buf.write(string, [offset], [length], [encoding]);`

> Writes indication into a buffer.

`buf.toString([encoding], [start], [end]);`

> Converts buffer data in indications. Standard for the coding is 'utf8', for *start* it is 0.

`buf.toJSON();`

> JSON representtion of the buffer contents.

`buf.copy(targetBuffer, [targetStart], [sourceStart], [sourceEnd]);`

> Copied between buffers.

`buf.slice([start], [end]);`

> Returns parts of a buffer.

`buf.fill(value, [offset], [end]);`

> Fills a buffer with firm values.

`buf[index];`

> The element at the index.

`buf.length;`

> Size of the buffer; contents do not have to use everything in the buffer.

`buffer.INSPECT_MAX_BYTES;`

> Maximum number of bytes, which return "buffer.inspect".

The API Reference for Express

The following reference explains systematically the functions of the Express module. It corresponds to a large extent to the original documentation, supplemental around further examples and background information.

Das Basic Objekt

The call express() produces an Express application. This is the module function, which was exported by the Express module.

```
1  var express = require('express');
2  var app = express();
```

The object Express has further methods.

Static Method of the Basic Object

The following syntax has this method:

```
express.static(root, [options])
```

This is a middleware function. It is the only one which you don't have to provide by yourself. This method defines master paths to folders in which static files are located. This concerns CSS, JavaScript or image files. This way you avoid building routes for such elements.

"root" points to the folder, whose contents are made available. The behavior can be affected by means of options:

Table A-1. *Options of the Function Static*

Property	Description	Type	St
dotfiles	Files, which begin with a dot. Permits values: "allow", "deny", "ignore"	String	"ignore"
etag	Produce "etag"	Boolean	True
extensions	Fallback for file extensions	Boolean	False
index	Index file for listing of the index or false for switching the list off	Mixed	"ignore"
lastModified	Puts on the header "Last-Modified" The file date of the operating system	Boolean	True
maxAge	Sets "max-age" of the header "Cache-Control" in milliseconds or a Character sequence of the kind "0ms"	Number	0
redirect	Bypass to the master path "/" if the path index is	Boolean	True
setHeaders	Function for setting the HTTP headers with sending the file	Function	

The following examples show, how "static" can be used. Here CSS files are expected in the folder */public*:

```
1   // GET /style.css etc
2   app.use(express.static(__dirname + '/public'));
```

Here the path *static* is connected in order to load files from the internal folder *public*:

```
1   // GET /static/style.css etc.
2   app.use('/static', express.static(__dirname + '/public'));
```

By calling the protocol object directly after the agreement of the static route, the logging for static files is switched off:

```
1   app.use(express.static(__dirname + '/public'));
2   app.use(logger());
```

If you distribute the static files on several folders, the call of "use" takes place several times. The sequence determines the search strategy:

```
1   app.use(express.static(__dirname + '/public'));
2   app.use(express.static(__dirname + '/files'));
3   app.use(express.static(__dirname + '/uploads'));
```

> **ℹ** **__dirname**   Node makes a global variable with the name dirname available. This always points to the path in which the currently implemented JavaScript file is. Thus, the local connection is made. '/', which is often comparably used, that shows the path in which Node is implemented. That can, but does not have to, be identical. Always use dirname for references within the application structure.

The application

Providing the application takes place on highest level. The production of an object usually has the name *App*.

Listing A-1. apphelloworld_sample.js

```
1   var express = require('express');
2   var app = express();
3
4   app.get('/', function(req, res){
5     res.send('hello world');
6   });
7
8   app.listen(3000);
```

The "app" object has methods for the following tasks:

- Routing
- Configuration of the Middleware
- Rendering of Views
- Registration of certain View Engines (e.g., Jade)

The "app" object also has features for configuration.

The Features of the Application Object

- app.locals

"app.locals" defines local variables specifically for the application and is permanently available. Examples:

- app.locals.title: Could be the title of the application.
- app.locals.email: Could be the E-Mail of the administrator.

The access to those variables can take place from all sides. The data is JavaScript objects, so that here maximum flexibility is present.

```
1   app.locals.title = 'My App';
2   app.locals.strftime = require('strftime');
3   app.locals.email = 'me@myapp.com';
```

- app.mountpath

The feature app.mountpath determines the sample of the path where a subordinated application is. Thus the routing of subordinated application parts is steered.

Listing A-2. mountpath_sample.js

```
1    var express = require('express');
2
3    var app = express();    // Main app
4    var admin = express(); // Sub app
5
6    admin.get('/', function (req, res) {
7      console.log(admin.mountpath); // Ausgabe des Stammpfades
8      res.send('Admin Homepage');
9    })
10
11   // Determine the root path of the sub app
12   app.use('/admin', admin);
```

The use of the method app.use provides for the link of application and router. Within the application you access these paths in order to dissolve, for example, relative references. That is comparable with the feature baseUrl of the requirement object '\'req.

If the subapplication should react to several paths (by path samples), app.mountpath will return a list with these paths (in form of a JavaScript array).

Listing A-3. mountpath2_sample.js

```
1    var admin = express();
2
3    admin.get('/', function (req, res) {
4        console.log(admin.mountpath); // [ '/adm*n', '/manager' ]
5        res.send('Admin Homepage');
6    })
7
8    var secret = express();
9    secret.get('/', function (req, res) {
10     console.log(secret.mountpath); // /secr*t
11     res.send('Admin Secret');
12   });
13
14   // Load the router 'secret' mit dem Pfad '/secre*'
15   // for the sub application admin
16   admin.use('/secre*', secret);
17
```

```
18    // Load the router 'admin' mit den Pfaden '/adm*' und '/manager'
19    // for the main application
20    app.use(['/adm*', '/manager'], admin);
```

In principle, regular expressions are processed if complex routes are defined. In JavaScript you write these in the literal spelling:

```
/\/adm(.*)/
```

The slash must be thereby masked '\/'. If you indicate routes in character strings, some special characters are intercepted and converted into suitable regular expressions. The following special characters are permitted:

- *: Zero or as many as desired indications

- • +: One or as many as desired indications

- ?: One or zero indications

- (): Group on which '*', '+' or '?' can be used

With character strings the indications '.' (dot) and '-' (minus) don't have a special meaning, but become part of the path.

```
1     // The fixed path /abcd
2     app.get('/abcd', function(req, res) {
3       res.send('abcd');
4     });
5
6     // The path /acd or /abcd
7     app.get('/ab?cd', function(req, res) {
8       res.send('ab?cd');
9     });
10
11    // The path /abbcd
12    // ('b' kann wiederholt werden)
13    app.get('/ab+cd', function(req, res) {
14      res.send('ab+cd');
15    });
16
17    // The path /abxyzcd
18    // (everything between 'b' and 'c' is allowed)
19    app.get('/ab*cd', function(req, res) {
20      res.send('ab*cd');
21    });
22
23    // The path /abe or /abcde matches
24    // ('cd' ist optional)
25    app.get('/ab(cd)?e', function(req, res) {
26      res.send('ab(cd)?e');
27    });
```

Consider the Sequence   Pay attention that weak routes will be defined last along with placeholders. Otherwise, all of these requests will intercept and concrete routes are never reached.

Combinations with parameters are interesting. Here in the path an intuitively usable range "of to" (e.g. */route/12-23*) is defined:

```
1   app.get('/route/:from-:to', function(req, res) {
2     res.send(req.params.from + ' to ' + req.params.to);
3   });
```

Likewise, a parameter can easily be made optional (line 1):

```
1   app.get('/feed/:format?', function(req, res) {
2     if (req.params.format) {
3       res.send('format: ' + req.params.format);
4     }
5     else {
6       res.send('default format');
7     }
8   });
```

The question mark makes the entire parameter optional. The inquiry in the code reacts to it (the value is undefined and this is in JavaScript false).

Regular expressions can certainly do more. The following route reacts to *pineapple, redapple, redaple, aaple* but not to *apple* and *apples*:

```
1   app.get(/.+app?le$/, function(req, res) {
2     res.send('/.+ap?le$/');
3   });
```

 Regular Expressions in Routes   If you don't have a good reason to use regular expressions, then you should stay with the character string spelling. Simpler routes are in the long term better controllable and often sufficient—parameters are responsible for the dynamics. However, if you should ever use regular expressions, then you absolutely need to use the literal spelling '//'.

Events

In Express, you can dynamically react to some procedures, which take place during the initialization. Thus program sections can be separated like the main and subapplications already mentioned, but more simply.

- `app.on('mount', callback(parent))`

This event arises, if a subapplication is bound to a main application. The superordinate application is then handed over as parameter.

Listing A-4. on_sample.js

```
1   var admin = express();
2
3   admin.on('mount', function (parent) {
4     console.log('Admin mounted');
5     console.log(parent); // parent app
6   });
7
8   admin.get('/', function (req, res) {
9     res.send('Admin Homepage');
10  });
11
12  // This call invokes an event
13  app.use('/admin', admin);
```

Methods of Application Level

Some further methods make fundamental functions available.

- app.all

This method receives a request and reacts to all HTTP verbs. The use of global methods relieves substantially the structure of flexible interfaces and avoids uselessly complex routes. Combine this method with a universal path sample as '*', in order to implement general tasks on all requests. It is important to understand which regular inquiring (instead of the use of the middleware) can work as intermediary. The request does not have to end compellingly with a result; it can also be passed on.

```
1   app.all('*', requireAuthentication, loadUser);
```

The parameters *requiredAuthentication* and *loadUser* will be executed one after another. The same call could be written like this:

```
1   app.all('*', requireAuthentication)
2   app.all('*', loadUser);
```

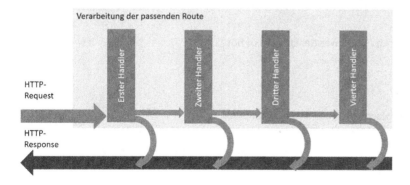

Figure A-1. *Several Callback Handler*

The difference is only stylistic. If you write the callback methods directly in the parameter, the second variant is clearer:

```
1  app.all('*', function(req, res) {
2    // Execute action
3  });
```

Likewise, more complex samples of paths can be provided in order to permit certain only global structures for the URL. If all paths start with /api, the following definition is suitable:

```
1  app.all('/api/*', requireAuthentication);
```

- app.delete

This method reacts to the HTTP Verb DELETE. It is used for the deletion of resources. It occurs usually only in connection with JavaScript Clients, which can send DELETE. Browsers alone cannot do this.

🔍 More Methods   You can use several methods for the same route. These are always successively implemented. Comparable methods of the middleware behave similarly, however, ignore the further processing steps.

```
1  app.delete('/', function (req, res) {
2    res.send('DELETE request to homepage');
3  });
```

- app.disable(name)

This method sets a feature of the central options to false. The call app.set('foo',false) leads to the same result.

```
1  app.disable('trust proxy');
2  app.get('trust proxy');
```

After this call the value shows false

- app.disabled(name)

This method checks whether an option was deactivated or not.

```
1  app.enable('trust proxy');
2  app.disabled('trust proxy');
```

Since first an activation took place, the second call shows true.

- **app.enable(name)**

  This method sets a feature of the central options to true. app.set('foo', true) leads to the same result.

```
1  app.enable('trust proxy');
2  app.get('trust proxy');
```

Since first an activation took place, the second call shows true.

- app.enabled(name)

This method checks whether an option was activated.

```
1  app.enable('trust proxy');
2  app.enabled('trust proxy');
```

Since first the activation took place, the second call shows true

- app.engine(ext, callback)

This method registers a View Engine. This is responsible for translating the special format from Views into valid HTML. Express finds the suitable engine according to standard automatically on the basis and the file extension of the View file. The name of the View file is for example *index.pug* implicitly that the Jade engine is used. The result is cached, so that the determination procedure won't be disturbed.

An explicit definition looks as follows:

```
1  app.engine('pug', require('pug').__express);
```

The call of the registration method does not always have to be " – express"0. The call could also look as follows:

```
1  app.engine('html', require('ejs').renderFile);
```

The module "EJS" offers a method renderFile for processing the View. However, the call is only necessary, because in this example the file extension *html* is used and not the standard *ejs* for the EJS engine.

Some Engines do not adhere to the call conventions. But there is the library *consolidate.js*, which can perform a translation from the Express-typical calls to the respective engine:

```
1  var engines = require('consolidate');
2  app.engine('haml', engines.haml);
3  app.engine('html', engines.hogan);
```

Q **What Engine?**   Due to simplicity and widespread use in this series of texts, the Pug engine will always be used as standard.

- app.get(name)

This form of the call returns an attitude.

```
1  app.get('title');
2
3  app.set('title', 'Mein StartUp');
4  app.get('title');
```

Here undefined (line 1) was produced, because *title* was not set yet. After the assignment with set (line 2), then the text "My StartUp" is shown (line 3).

Caution with Get   Do not confuse this syntax with the use of "get" as action.

- `app.get`

This method reacts to requests with the HTTP Verb GET. If such a request is received over the indicated route, the callback method is successively implemented.

More Methods   You can use several methods for the same route. These are always successively implemented. Comparable methods of the middleware behave similarly, however they can ignore the further processing steps.

```
1   app.get('/', function (req, res) {
2     res.send('GET-Anfrage empfangen');
3   });
```

- app.listen

This method binds a port and then begins to listen. The call is an abbreviation for the Node method "listen()" and corresponds there "http.Server.listen()".

```
1   var express = require('express');
2   var app = express();
3   app.listen(3000);
```

The application which is provided by Express is a function in its core, which is handed over to Node. Node regards these as callback methods and calls it with arriving requests. Thus the data from Node arrives to Express. Since it concerns only a callback method, the application object can be used several times. In the following example, the connection takes place twice, once for HTTP and once for HTTPS:

Listing A-5. listen_sample.js

```
1   var express = require('express');
2   var https = require('https');
3   var http = require('http');
4   var app = express();
5
6   http.createServer(app).listen(80);
7   https.createServer(app).listen(443);
```

The following variant defines the server implicitly over "this":

```
1   app.listen = function() {
2     var server = http.createServer(this);
3     return server.listen.apply(server, arguments);
4   };
```

Further variants are to be found in the documentation of Node.js or in Jörgs small Web band to Node.

More Methods

As shown in the preceding examples already, Express reacts to HTTP verbs by a suitable method. In principle, all theoretically conceivable HTTP verbs are available as method. While in HTTP the verbs are always located in capital letters, these always are small letters in JavaScript methods. The HTTP verb HEAD is thus processed by the method app.head().

Express knows the following methods:

- checkout: For WebDAV for closing resources

- Connect: Structure of the connection

- copy: For WebDAV for duplicating resources

- delete: Deletes a resource on the server

- get: Regular requirement of resources without payload in the request

- head: Like get, however the client expects only headers back

- lock: For WebDAV for blocking resources

- merge: For REST for connecting data

- mkactivity: For WebDAV for the creation of an activity

- mkcol: For WebDAV for producing a collection

- move: For WebDAV for shifting resources

- m-search: Search for Resources

- notify: Notification

- options: To determine options and requirements of the server

- patch: Change a part of resources

- post: Regular requirement of resources with payload in the request. Produces a new Data record with REST (insert)

- propfind: For WebDAV for determining resources

- proppatch: For WebDAV for looking and changing of a resource

- purge: Final removing of resources

- put: Only for REST; contains a payload and changes resources (update)

- report: Report on the structure of resources

- search: For WebDAV for looking for resources

- subscribe: For WebDAV for connecting with resources

- trace: Loop back on the server for pursuing processing

- unlock: For WebDAV for releasing blocked resources

- unsubscribe: For WebDAV for waiving the connection with resources

Names which do not show a valid spelling in JavaScript can be reached by means of the clip spelling:

```
1    app['m-search']('/', function ....
```

> ℹ **About the Sense or Nonsense of Many Verbs**   There is some criticism about the complexity and variety of the verbs, particularly, some by special extensions such as WebDAV or CalDAV that were added. There are quite complex applications, which are only based on GET and POST. In addition, the implementation is somewhat complex because each of the verbs can return many different status codes and become communication partial comprehensive XML structures, as expected. Do like the K.I.S.S. concept says and implement only verbs which are really needed. You should use these only standard-conformal.

Meaningful verbs for browsers are:

- GET: Get data from the server
- POST: Send data to the server

Meaningful verbs for REST are:

- GET: Read resources
- POST: Produce resources
- PUT: Change resources
- PATCH: Change parts of resources
- DELETE: Delete resources

Each method processes several callback methods, which are indicated as individual parameters. These methods process three parameters:

- req: The Request (request)
- res: The Answer (response)
- next: A method which is called to continue processing.

The names of the parameters are arbitrary; however, the shown names worked because of catchyness and their shortness.

```
1    app.all('/secret', function (req, res, next) {
2      console.log('Called secret function ...')
3      next(); // Let's go on...
4    });
```

```
1    app.post('/', function (req, res) {
2      res.send('POST Request');
3    });
```

```
1   app.put('/', function (req, res) {
2     res.send('PUT Request');
3   });
```

- app.param

This method adds to determined parameters, which are part of a route. Callback functions in addition process these methods as four parameters:

- req: The Request (request)

- res: The Answer(response)

- next: A method which is called to continue processing

- param: The parameter value

If now a route with the name *:user* is located inside a parameter, the callback method would react to it, **before** the actual action of the route is implemented.

```
1   app.param('user', function(req, res, next, id) {
2
3     // Fiktives "User"-Objekt
4     User.find(id, function(err, user) {
5       if (err) {
6         next(err);
7       } else if (user) {
8         req.user = user;
9         next();
10      } else {
11        next(new Error('failed to load user'));
12      }
13    });
14  });
```

The treatment of the parameter is local for the router, where they were defined. The parameters are not left over, connected application parts. The callback method is called only once within a requirement answer cycle, even if the parameter is used by several routes.

```
1   app.param('id', function (req, res, next, id) {
2     console.log('Called once');
3     next();
4   })
5
6   app.get('/user/:id', function (req, res, next) {
7     console.log('Will be reached');
8     next();
9   });
10
11  app.get('/user/:id', function (req, res) {
12    console.log('And this, too');
13    res.end();
14  });
```

The last part terminates the request eventually.

- `app.render`

This method serves the rendering of a View. The name of the View can be indicated without file extension. The parameter `local` is optional and is used in order to hand over the View local varable.

That finished, the rendered HTML is sent over the callback function.

There is a local variable with the name "cache", which ensures that the View becomes buffered. At the draft this time is `false`; at the production time, it is `true`. Set the value in order to reach another behavior at the draft time.

```
1   app.render('email', function(err, html) {
2     // ...
3   });
```

A View with the name *email.jade* is loaded (if Pug is used).

Then this is rendered. In the callback function "html" contains the rendered View as character string. This can be handed over to the server, so that it continues to deliver it to the client.

The call of `res.render()` in the actions of the router is internally calling `app.render()`.

Local variables for the View can be handed over via the object:

```
1   app.render('email', { name: 'Joerg' }, function(err, html){
2     // ...
3   });
```

- `app.route(path)`

With this method, the individual route object is returned. With this HTTP, verbs can be treated—with or without middleware. By the use of objects you can avoid typing errors in character strings.

Listing A-6. route_sample.js

```
1   var app = express();
2
3   app.route('/events')
4     .all(function(req, res, next) {
5       // All Methods
6     })
7     .get(function(req, res, next) {
8       // nur GET
9       res.json(...);
10    })
11    .post(function(req, res, next) {
12      // nur POST
13    });
```

- app.set(name, value)

This method sets features for the application.

```
1   app.set('title', 'My StartUp');
2   app.get('title');
```

The following table describes the available features.

Table A-2. *Features*

Features	Typ	Description	Default
case sensitive routing	Boolean	Capitalization in routes	false
env	String	Environment mode, NODE_ENV or "development"	process.env.NODE_ENV
etag	Varied	ETag Header	
jsonp callback	String	JSONP callback name	?callback=
json replacer	String	JSON replacer callback	null
json spaces	Number	Indention in JSON	none
query parser	String	"simple" or "extended"	"simple" = Node; "extend
strict routing	Boolean	Striktes Routing	false
subdomain offset	Number	Points in Subdomain path	2
trust proxy	Varied	See below	false
views	String	Array	Folder with Views
view cache	Boolean	Compiler Cache	true in the production
view engine	String	Engine for Views	
x-powered-by	Boolean	"X-Powered-By: Express"	true

With the routes the upper and lower cases are not differentiated. However, if the value *case sensitive routing* is true, "/Foo" and "/foo" won't be the same anymore. With *strict routing* the concluding, theoretically ineffective, Slash won't be ignored, if the value stands on true; "/foo" and "/foo/" are then not the same.

trust proxy is, according to standard, switched off. If it were activated, Express tries to determine the IP address of the clients by the proxy. The feature req.ips contains thereafter an array with IP addresses by which the client is connected. The package, as this implementation puts it, is called *proxy_addr*. Further information is to be found in the documentation of this package:

The options for trust proxy settings are the following:

- Boolean: With true, the IP address of the client is "X-Forwarded-*" as the part on the furthest left of the headers. With "false", the client is assumed to be directly connected with the internet and the IP address comes out of "eq.connection. remoteAddress". This is the standard attitude.

- IP address: An IP address, a subnet or an array from IP addresses and subnets which is trusted. Some are already preconfigured:

  - *loopback* – 127.0.0.1/8, ::1/128

  - *linklocal* – 169.254.0.0/16, fe80::/10

  - *uniquelocal* – 10.0.0.0/8, 172.16.0.0/12, 192.168.0.0/16, fc00::/7

Set the IP address as follows:

```
1   // Simple subnet
2   app.set('trust proxy', 'loopback')
3   // subnet and address
4   app.set('trust proxy', 'loopback, 8.8.8.8')
5   // multiple subnets
6   app.set('trust proxy', 'loopback, linklocal, uniquelocal')
7   // multiple subnets as array
8   app.set('trust proxy', ['loopback', 'linklocal', 'uniquelocal'])
```

If indicated, the addresses and subnets become excluded by the address evaluation and the not-trusted address, which is closest to the server seized as the IP address of the client.

- Number: Trust the ninth Hop from the Proxy to the Client.

- Function: An own implementation by means of a callback function.

```
1   app.set('trust proxy', function (ip) {
2       if (ip === '127.0.0.1' || ip === '123.123.123.123') return true;\
3   // trusted IPs
4       else return false;
5   })
```

The options for etag settings are just as various:

- Boolean: true permits a weak ETag. This is the standard. false turns the ETag completely off.

- String: If the value strong was used, then this turns on a strong ETag. Weak, however, produces a weak ETag.

- Function: An own implementation by means of a callback function.

ⓘ ETag The ETag (entity tag) is a header field introduced to HTTP 1.1. It serves the avoidance of redundant data transfer for the regulation resources requested by changes at and mainly for the caching; this is how it is used.

```
1   app.set('etag', function (body, encoding) {
2       return generateHash(body, encoding); // consider the function is d\
3   efined
4   })
```

- app.use

With this method, middleware functions are added to a route. If the path is not indicated, the root '/' is used. Routes are search samples, which also fulfill partial conditions. The path app.use('/app',...) will also react to */apple, /apple/images, /apple/images/news,* etc.

Use the feature `req.originalUrl` in order to receive the complete path:

```
1   app.use('/admin', function(req, res, next) {
2     // GET 'http://www.example.com/admin/new'
3     console.log(req.originalUrl); // '/admin/new'
4     console.log(req.baseUrl); // '/admin'
5     console.log(req.path); // '/new'
6     next();
7   });
```

If the middleware function is bound, it will always be called, if a valid route is requested, independently on the further processing. If you bind the root, the function is called practically with each requirement. Pay attention to performance-critical actions, because in such a central place a small programming error can have significant effects.

```
1   app.use(function (req, res, next) {
2     console.log('Time: %d', Date.now());
3     next();
4   });
```

Middleware functions are sequentially implemented. The sequence of the definition determines the order of the execution. If the call `next()` is missing, then the execution stops here:

```
1   app.use(function(req, res, next) {
2     res.send('Hello World');
3   });
4   // Diese Aktion wird niemals erreicht
5   app.get('/', function (req, res) {
6     res.send('Welcome');
7   })
```

The path can be a character string, a path sample (see below), a regular expression, or a combination of them. Simple paths are indicated directly:

```
1   app.use('/abcd', function (req, res, next) {
2     next();
3   });
```

- Path sample

Path samples use placeholders:

```
1   app.use('/abc?d', function (req, res, next) {
2     next();
3   });
```

The question mark makes an indication optional. Suitable paths would be */abcxd* or */abcd*. The plus sign stands for yes or several occurrences (*/abcd, /abbcd, /abbbbbcd*):

```
1   app.use('/ab+cd', function (req, res, next) {
2     next();
3   });
```

161

The asterisk stands for no or several occurrences of arbitrary indications (*/abcd*, */abxcd*, */abFOOcd*, / *abbArcd* etc.):

```
1  app.use('/ab\*cd', function (req, res, next) {
2    next();
3  });
```

Blocks can be made optional by grouping (*/ad* and */abcd*):

```
1  app.use('/a(bc)?d', function (req, res, next) {
2    next();
3  });
```

- Regular Expressions

The following path reacts to */abc* and */xyz*:

```
1  app.use(/\/abc|\/xyz/, function (req, res, next) {
2    next();
3  });
```

In addition, several arrays can be used. Consider that chracter strings and literal ones for regular expressions can be mixed here (even if this is no such a good idea):

```
1  app.use(['/abcd', '/xyza', /\/lmn|\/pqr/],
2        function (req, res, next) {
3    next();
4  });
```

- The Callback Function

By the information of one or more callback functions the access to the requirement and the object is possible, in which the answer is designed.

```
1  app.use(function (req, res, next) {
2    next();
3  });
```

The router itself is also a middleware function and uses the same signature:

```
1  var router = express.Router();
2  router.get('/', function (req, res, next) {
3    next();
4  })
5  app.use(router);
```

The application itself can also be used:

```
1  var subApp = express();
2  subApp.get('/', function (req, res, next) {
3    next();
4  })
5  app.use(subApp);
```

Further Callback Functions

The same path can serve several middleware functions.

```
1   var r1 = express.Router();
2   r1.get('/', function (req, res, next) {
3       next();
4   })
5
6   var r2 = express.Router();
7   r2.get('/', function (req, res, next) {
8     next();
9   })
10
11  app.use(r1, r2);
```

Alternatively, objects can be indicated as arrays and this way be grouped logically. Here the master path must be indicated as:

```
1   var r1 = express.Router();
2   r1.get('/', function (req, res, next) {
3     next();
4   })
5
6   var r2 = express.Router();
7   r2.get('/', function (req, res, next) {
8     next();
9   })
10
11  app.use('/', [r1, r2]);
```

Combinations

You can combine all described parameters.

```
1   function mw1(req, res, next) { next(); }
2   function mw2(req, res, next) { next(); }
3
4   var r1 = express.Router();
5   r1.get('/', function (req, res, next) { next(); });
6
7   var r2 = express.Router();
8   r2.get('/', function (req, res, next) { next(); });
9
10  var subApp = express();
11  subApp.get('/', function (req, res, next) { next(); });
12
13  app.use(mw1, [mw2, r1, r2], subApp);
```

Request–The Request Object

In many preceding examples, the parameter "req" was made available by Express. It concerns a Request object. You can access all components of the requirement, their parameter, the QueryString, etc.

```
1  app.get('/user/:id', function(req, res){
2    res.send('user ' + req.params.id);
3  });
```

Q The name "req" is used in all examples because it is short and catchy. You do not have to use these names; it is only a parameter of a regular JavaScript function.

The Features

- `req.app`

This is the instance of the application
Define as example the following in the file *index.js*:

```
1  app.get("/viewdirectory", require("./mymiddleware.js"))
```

In another file *mymiddleware.js* will then access the application object, even though *app* isn't available anymore:

```
1  module.exports = function (req, res) {
2    res.send("The views directory is " + req.app.get("views"));
3  });
```

Here a middleware function is exported. It then receives the same parameters as the regular functions of the router.

- `req.baseUrl`

This feature shows the basic path of the router instance:

```
1  var greet = express.Router();
2
3  greet.get('/jp', function (req, res) {
4    console.log(req.baseUrl); // /greet
5    res.send('Konichiwa!');
6  });
7
8  app.use('/greet', greet); // Load router for '/greet'
```

If path samples or regular expressions are used for the definition of the paths, this feature returns the final, complete path, no sample.

```
1  app.use(['/gre+t', '/hel{2}o'], greet);
2  console.log(req.baseUrl); // => /greet.
```

The code in line 1 defines the routes for *gre+t* and *hel{2}o*.

- `req.body`

Contains key pair values of the data of the body range. This is according to standard "undefined and fulfilled by middleware functions. How this looks is shown in the following example:

```
1   var app = require('express')();
2   var bodyParser = require('body-parser');
3   var multer = require('multer');
4
5   // for parsing application/json
6   app.use(bodyParser.json());
7   // for parsing application/x-www-form-urlencoded
8   app.use(bodyParser.urlencoded({ extended: true }));
9
10  app.use(multer()); // for parsing multipart/form-data
11
12  app.post('/', function (req, res) {
13    console.log(req.body);
14    res.json(req.body);
15  });
```

- `req.cookies`

If cookies are processed, this feature contains an object of the cookies contained in the request. Standard is an empty '{}' object.

```
1   // Cookie: name=tj
2   req.cookies.name // => "tj"
```

The module *cookie-parser* supplies functionality.

- `req.fresh`

A boolean value shows that the request is "fresh" (up-to-date, intact). The opposite of it is "req.stale". The condition is that the head field *cache-control* has no "no-cache" directive and any of the following conditions entered:

- The head field *if-modified-since* is present and *last-modified* is the same or as earlier

- The head fielld *if-none-match* is *.

- The head field *if-none-match* contains no ETag.

- req.hostname

Contains the host name, as it is located in the head field *Host* of the request.

```
1   // Host: "example.com:3000"
2   req.hostname
```

- `req.ip`

The IP address, to which the request was sent. The value can differ from the server, if Proxies are used.

```
1   req.ip // => "127.0.0.1"
```

- req.ips

Contains the addresses of head field *X-Forwarded-For* as array or an empty array, if the field is not used.

- req.originalUrl

Contains the original URL. You can overwrite "reg-url" internally, in order to steer the routing dynamically. In such cases the previous value remains nevertheless in "req.originalUrl".

```
1   // GET /search?q=something
2   req.originalUrl
3   // => "/search?q=something"
```

- req.params

An object with the parameters of the route. If the route is */article/:id*, for example, then the value for *:id* will be found in the feature "req.params.id". Without parameters an empty object can be found '{}'.

```
1   // GET /article/2605
2   req.params.id // => 2605
```

If in the definition of the route regular expressions are used, the recognized groups (capture groups) are returned as array of the object: "req.params[n]". *n* is thereby the number of the group. This is also valid for placeholders in routes, such as */file/**:

```
1   // GET /file/javascripts/jquery.js
2   req.params[0]
3   // => "javascripts/jquery.js"
```

- req.path

  Contains the path information of the URL, that is, the part after the host and before the QueryString.

```
1   // example.com/users?sort=desc
2   req.path
3   // => "/users"
```

- req.protocol

  The protocol (or pattern), thus "http" or "https".

```
1   req.protocol // => "http"
```

- req.query

An object with the QueryString parameters. If these are missing, an empty object '{}' is returned.

```
1   // GET /search?q=joerg+krause
2   req.query.q
3   // Ergibt => "joerg krause"
4
5   // GET /shoes?order=desc&shoe[color]=blue
6   req.query.order
7   // Ergibt => "desc"
8
9   req.query.shoe.color
10  // Ergibt => "blue"
```

- req.route

Contains the current, suitable route as character string.

```
1   app.get('/user/:id?', function userIdHandler(req, res) {
2     console.log(req.route);
3     res.send('GET');
4   })
```

The output of the information as JSON object now looks as follows:

```
1   { path: '/user/:id?',
2     stack:
3     [ { handle: [Function: userIdHandler],
4         name: 'userIdHandler',
5         params: undefined,
6         path: undefined,
7         keys: [],
8         regexp: /^\/?$/i,
9         method: 'get' } ],
10    methods: { get: true }
11  }
```

- req.secure

A boolean value, which shows that it concerns a coded connection (TLS, represented as "https"). The following inquiry is equivalent:

```
"https" == req.protocol;
```

- req.signedCookies

If cookies are processed, this feature contains signed cookies. This is only an announcement for the developer that this cookie serves a special purpose. They are neither coded nor hidden. The signature is *private* and prevented from access with an attack on the cookie object.

```
1   // Cookie: user=joerg.IT7AWaXDfAKIRfH26dQzKJx05sKzzSoPq64
2   req.signedCookies.user
3   // Ergibt => "joerg"
```

- req.stale

The request is not valid any longer. The feature returns "true" or "false".

- req.subdomains

The array of the subdomain in the request.

```
1   // Host: "joerg.admin.texxtoor.com"
2   req.subdomains
3   // => ["admin", "joerg"]
```

- req.xhr

A boolean value shows that the field *X-Requested-With* is used and contains the value "XMLHttpRequest". Thus, AJAX calls are recognized. The field is used among other things by the client library jQuery. The feature returns "true" or "false".

Methods

- req.accepts(types)

This method checks whether the requested content types are accepted or not. The requirement takes place with the head field *accept*. The return value should be *406 "Not Acceptable"*, if content types are not accepted.

The values are MIME types, as for example 'application/json', or also extensions such as 'json'. Several values can be separated by comma.

```
1   // Accept: text/html
2   req.accepts('html');
3   // => "html"
4
5   // Accept: text/*, application/json
6   req.accepts('html');
7   // => "html"
8   req.accepts('text/html');
9   // => "text/html"
10  req.accepts(['json', 'text']);
11  // => "json"
12  req.accepts('application/json');
13  // => "application/json"
14
15  // Accept: text/*, application/json
16  req.accepts('image/png');
17  req.accepts('png');
18  // => undefined
19
20  // Accept: text/*;q=.5, application/json
21  req.accepts(['html', 'json']);
22  // => "json"
```

- req.acceptsCharsets

Evaluates the field "Accept-Charset". If nothing is recognized, "false" is produced. Syntax:

```
req.acceptsCharsets(charset [, ...])
```

- req.acceptsEncodings

Evaluates the field "Accept-Encoding". If nothing is recognized, "false" is produced. Syntax:

```
req.acceptsEncodings(encoding [, ...])
```

- req.acceptsLanguages

Evaluates the field "Accept-Language". If nothing is recognized, "false" is produced. Syntax:

```
req.acceptsLanguages(lang [, ...])
```

- req.get(field)

Evaluates the indicated field. Upper and lower cases are not considered. The terms *Referer* and *Referrer* are exchangeable.

ℹ Referrer with two 'r' is the correct name. The fact that Referer is also possible is justified because an early version of the standardization document (RFC 2068) contained a write error and so the standard raised the wrong spelling.

```
1    req.get('Content-Type');
2    // => "text/plain"
3
4    req.get('content-type');
5    // => "text/plain"
6
7    req.get('Something');
8    // => undefined
9    Aliased as req.header(field).
```

- req.is(type)

Returns true, if the field "Content-Type" corresponds to the parameter value.
If "Content-Type: text/html; charset=utf-8" was received, true arises:

```
1    req.is('html');
2    req.is('text/html');
3    req.is('text/*');
```

If "Content-Type: application/json" was received, true arises:

```
1    req.is('json');
2    req.is('application/json');
3    req.is('application/*');
```

The same request turned out to be "false" for this call:

```
1   req.is('html');
```

Response–The Answer Object

The response is arranged in the object 'res'. This is used to send data to the client.

ℹ The name res   The designation of the object is arbitrary; however, in the original documentation and in this book this name is used throughout.

```
1   app.get('/user/:id', function(req, res){
2     res.send('user ' + req.params.id);
3   });
```

The same inquiry could look as follows:

```
1   app.get('/user/:id', function(request, response){
2     response.send('user ' + request.params.id);
3   });
```

Features

- `res.app`

This feature supplies a reference to the instance of the application.
This reference is identical to the same feature as in the Request object.

- `res.headersSent`

A boolean value, which shows that the head fields were actually sent. After this point of time no further head fields can be produced and sent.

```
1   app.get('/', function (req, res) {
2     console.log(res.headersSent); // false
3     res.send('OK');
4     console.log(res.headersSent); // true
5   })
```

- `res.locals`

Local variables, which are only available for the current requirement/inquiry cycle. Thus, data can be transported into a View. This differs from "app.locals" only to the extent that in "app.locals", existing variables in all requests are available.

This feature is useful in order to pass information on from the requirement to the View.

```
1   app.use(function(req, res, next){
2     res.locals.user = req.user;
3     res.locals.authenticated = ! req.user.anonymous;
4     next();
5   });
```

Methods

- res.append

Adds a value to a head field. If the field does not exist yet, then it is now produced. The values can be character sequences or arrays. Syntax:

```
res.append(field [, value])
```

 If "res.set()" is used after "res.append()", then the former value is put back.

```
1   res.append('Link', ['<http://localhost/>', '<http://localhost:3000/>\
2   ']);
3   res.append('Set-Cookie', 'foo=bar; Path=/; HttpOnly');
4   res.append('Warning', '199 Miscellaneous warning');
```

- res.attachment

If the field "Content-Disposition" sets to the value "attachment". If the file name is indicated, then also the part "filename=parameter" is set. This serves to animate the browser to offer data for downloading. Syntax:

```
res.attachment([filename])
```

```
1   res.attachment();
2   // Content-Disposition: attachment
3
4   res.attachment('path/to/logo.png');
5   // Content-Disposition: attachment; filename="logo.png"
6   // Content-Type: image/png
```

- res.cookie

Sets the name of a cookie. The value can be a character sequence or an object. If it is an object, this is converted in JSON. Syntax:

```
res.cookie(name, value [, options])
```

The options are described below:

Table A-3. *Cookie Options*

Property	Type	Description
domain	String	Domain name for the cookie. The domain name of the app is standard.
expires	Date	Expiration date of the cookies in GMT. If here nothing is indicated, 0 is.
httpOnly	Boolean	Marks a cookie, so that it is read only on the server.
maxAge	String	An option, in order to set the expiration date relative to the current time.
path	String	Path of the cookies; the standard is "/".
secure	Boolean	It specifies that the cookie is only supplied over HTTPS.
signed	Boolean	It specifies that the cookie must always be signed.

Cookies are packets, which are sent as head fields. The function "res.cookie()" produces such a head field with the indicated options. If an option is not indicated, then the in RFC 6265 indicated a default value is used.

```
1   res.cookie('name', 'joerg', {
2               domain: '.texxtoor.com',
3               path: '/admin', secure: true
4           });
5   res.cookie('remember', '1', {
6               expires: new Date(Date.now() + 60000),
7               httpOnly: true
8           });
```

The option *maxAge* uses one time interval for the expiration date relatively for the time of delivering. The following example will produce the same cookie as the last example:

```
1   res.cookie('rememberme', '1', { maxAge: 60000, httpOnly: true })
```

If JSON objects are handed over to the cookie function, then these are parsed and placed as serialized JSON in the cookie.

```
1   res.cookie('cart', { items: [1,2,3] });
2   res.cookie('cart', { items: [1,2,3] }, { maxAge: 900000 });
```

The function also supports signed cookies. The function produces a secret Hash automatically for the signature.

```
1   res.cookie('name', 'tobi', { signed: true });
```

Over "req.signedCookie", the cookie is then accessed later on. The middleware checks the signature and recognizes manipulations on the cookie.

The following method deletes a cookie by indicating the name:

```
1   res.clearCookie(name [, options])
```

```
1   res.cookie('name', 'joerg', { path: '/admin' });
2   res.clearCookie('name', { path: '/admin' });
```

- res.download

This method offers a file for downloading. This takes place via producing a suitable head field *Content-Disposition*. If the file name is indicated, the value is supplemented over *filename=filename*. The path parameter refers to the source of the file. The callback function *fn* serves to show success or failure of the procedure; it is called at the end of the transmission and contains HTTP status codes. Internally. `res.sendFile()` is used for the transmission of the file. Syntax:

```
res.download(path [, filename] [, fn])
```

```
1    res.download('/report-2605.pdf');
2
3    res.download('/report-2605.pdf', 'report.pdf');
4
5    res.download('/report-2605.pdf', 'report.pdf',
6                function(err){
7                    if (err) {
8                        // Fehler
9                    } else {
10                       // Erfolg
11                   }
12               });
```

With the treatment of errors (line 6), it is to be noted that an output of error message possibly fails the user, since other head fields were already dispatched. Check with `res.headersSent` if the sending of data is still possible.

- res.end

This method terminates the answer procedure. The call is useful for the Node core, especially `response.end()` of the object `http.ServerResponse`. Syntax:

```
res.end([data] [, encoding])
```

This is meaningful, if a request is to be terminated immediately without data.

```
1   res.end();
2   res.status(404).end();
```

- res.format

This method tries to read the head field "*Accept*" and then decide, how a response should be formatted. In addition `req.accepts()` is called. If the head field does not exist, the first callback function is used. If there is no editing, the *406 "Not Acceptable"* is produced. If a standard callback function is available, this is used. Syntax:

```
res.format(object)
```

If a callback function is used, the head field *Content-Type* will be produced along with the response. This behavior can be changed by using `res.set()` or `res.type()`.

The following example produces the JSON serialization {`message: hello`}, if the *Accept* head field contains the MIME type "application/json" or "*/json". Otherwise only the text "hello" will be output. However, if HTML is requested explicitly(MIME type is 'text/html'), <p>hello</p> is produced.

```
1   res.format({
2     'text/plain': function(){
3       res.send('hallo');
4     },
5
6     'text/html': function(){
7       res.send('<p>hallo</p>');
8     },
9
10    'application/json': function(){
11      res.send({ message: 'hallo' });
12    },
13
14    'default': function() {
15      // log the request and respond with 406
16      res.status(406).send('Not Acceptable');
17    }
18  });
```

As an alternative to the character string representation of the MIME types, mapping can be used in different methods, which is somewhat less complex and error-prone:

```
1   res.format({
2     text: function(){
3       res.send('hallo');
4     },
5
6     html: function(){
7       res.send('<p>hallo</p>');
8     },
9
10    json: function(){
11      res.send({ message: 'hallo' });
12    }
13  });
```

- res.get

This method returns a certain head field, designated by the parameter *field*. Syntax:
res.get(field)

```
1   res.get('Content-Type');
2   // Resolves to "text/plain"
```

- res.json

This method sends a JSON response. Each data type can be used, not only JavaScript objects, but also "zero" or "undefined". Syntax:

res.json([body])

```
1   res.json(null)
2   res.json({ user: 'joerg' })
3   res.status(500).json({ error: 'message' })
```

- res.jsonp

This is a JSON response with JSONP support. This corresponds to the preceding method, however with acceptance of JSONP. Syntax:

res.jsonp([body])

 JSONP JSONP (JSON with Padding) makes the transmission of JSON data possible over domain borders. Usually Ajax data inquiries are at servers over the XMLHttpRequest object of the browser. A security concept, the *Same-Origin-Policy* prevents that parts of a webpage are loaded by different servers. This prevents stranger scripts or CSS from being transferred. However, if a server environment scales, then pictures or scripts are possibly consciously loaded from another server. Such inquiries are permissible, if JSONP is used. The inquiry is packed in a <script> tag, which is exceptional by definition from *Same-Origin-Policy*.

```
1   res.jsonp(null)
2   // => null
3
4   res.jsonp({ user: 'joerg' })
5   // => { "user": "joerg" }
6
7   res.status(500).jsonp({ error: 'message' })
8   // => { "error": "message" }
```

The JSONP callback function is a simple JavaScript callback function according to standard. However, this can be modified.

```
1   // ?callback=foo
2   res.jsonp({ user: 'joerg' })
3   // ergibt foo({ "user": "joerg" })
4
5   app.set('jsonp callback name', 'cb');
```

```
6
7    // ?cb=foo
8    res.status(500).jsonp({ error: 'message' })
9    // ergibt foo({ "error": "message" })
```

In the client code, the exemplary method "foo" should be found; with it other domain-loaded data can be processed.

- `res.links`

This method connects the parameter presented hyperlinks and produces the head field *Link*. Syntax:

```
res.links(links)
```

ℹ **The Link Head Field**   *Link* is used in order to communicate the client further files or resources, e.g. a RSS feed, a Fav icon, copyright licenses, etc. This head field is equivalent to `<link/>` in HTML.

```
1    res.links({
2      next: 'http://api.example.com/users?page=2',
3      last: 'http://api.example.com/users?page=5'
4    });
```

This shows in the HTTP:

```
1    Link: <http://api.example.com/users?page=2>; rel="next",
2          <http://api.example.com/users?page=5>; rel="last"
```

- `res.location`

This method produces the *Location* head field. Syntax:

```
res.location(path)
```

ℹ **Location**   *Location* is often used in order to pass Clients on (with a 3xx Code).

```
1    res.location('/foo/bar');
2    res.location('foo/bar');
3    res.location('http://example.com');
4    res.location('../login');
5    res.location('back');
```

The information of the path corresponds to those with *redirect*. See in addition the following method.

- `res.redirect`

This method also produces a *Location* head field. It does not take place an examination or a contral, whether the value is meaningful or executable. The only exception is the value "back". Syntax:

```
res.redirect([status,] path)
```

The browser is responsible in some instances to arrange the final path of the actual page and the relevant entries, in order to bypass and execute it. Rerouting is initiated by the status code 302. Other codes are possible, but would then have to be named explicitly. A complete instruction for bypass consists thus of the request for bypass 302 and then instruction for the bypass *Location*.

```
1  res.redirect('/foo/bar');
2  res.redirect('http://example.com');
3  res.redirect(301, 'http://example.com');
4  res.redirect('../login');
```

Paths relative to others are also possible:

```
1  res.redirect('..');
```

The special value "back" uses the requirement head field *Referrer* for bypass on the preceding page. If this head field is not found, '/' will be used on the master path.

```
1  res.redirect('back');
```

- `res.render`

This method renders (provides) a View and sends the finished HTML to the client. Syntax:

```
res.render(view [, locals] [, callback])
```

The optional parameters have the following meaning:

- `locals`: An object, over which local variables can be handed over at Views. A callback function, over which the access to error information or the rendered View as character string exists. Sending the rendered data does not take place automatically. In the event of an error, `next()` is called internally, in order to guarantee the further processing.

Without callback function, the rendered View is sent directly to the client.

```
res.render('index');
```

With callback function, the rendered View is returned and must be sent with `send`.

```
1  res.render('index', function(err, html) {
2    res.send(html);
3  });
```

Local variables are expected as objects:

```
1  res.render('user', { name: 'Tobi' }, function(err, html) {
2    // ...
3  });
```

- res.send

This method sends an HTTP answer. Syntax:

```
res.send([body])
```

This method expects either a buffer, a character string, a JavaScript object or an array:

```
1  res.send(new Buffer('whoop'));
2  res.send({ message: 'json' });
3  res.send('<p>Etwas HTML</p>');
4  res.status(404).send('Not found!');
5  res.status(500).send({ error: 'Error while executing' });
```

If neither of the answer is determined and the suitable head field *Content-Length* is produced. In addition, cache information is updated and administered. If the parameter is recognized as buffer object buffers, the value "application/octet-stream" will be produced as MIME type in the head field *Content-Type*. This automatically can be skipped as follows:

```
1  res.set('Content-Type', 'text/html');
2  res.send(new Buffer('<p>Etwas HTML</p>'));
```

With HTML, the head field *Content-Type* is set to "text/html":

```
1  res.send('<p>some html</p>');
```

An array or an object is interpreted as JSON:

```
1  res.send({ user: 'joerg' });
2  res.send([1,2,3]);
```

- res.sendFile

This functions sends a file, which was loaded by the indicated path. Based on the file extension the head field *Content-Type* is set. Note that this does not lead necessarily to downloading the file, but the answer on its way as regular response to the browser. Syntax:

```
res.sendFile(path [, options] [, fn])
```

The options are described in the following.

Table A-4. *Options of the function sendFile*

Property	Description
maxAge	Sets the feature "max-age" of the head field cache control in ms or as character
root	The master directory for relative file names
lastModified	Sets the head field "Last-Modified" to the date of the last change of the file, as the
headers	Further HTTP head fields
dotfiles	Options for files, which start with a dot: "allow", "deny", "ignore". The value 'ign

The method uses a callback function which is called if the transfer took place. If an error arose, this must be treated explicitly. This takes place either via direct providing and sending of the response or via explicit terminating of the procedure or via passing on to the next route.

```
1    app.get('/file/:name', function (req, res, next) {
2
3      var options = {
4        root: __dirname + '/public/',
5        dotfiles: 'deny',
6        headers: {
7            'x-timestamp': Date.now(),
8            'x-sent': true
9        }
10     };
11
12     var fileName = req.params.name;
13     res.sendFile(fileName, options, function (err) {
14       If (err) {
15         console.log(err);
16         res.status(err.status).end();
17       }
18       else {
19         console.log('Sent:', fileName);
20       }
21     });
22
23   })
```

res.sendFile makes different exact reactions possible:

```
1    app.get('/user/:uid/photos/:file', function(req, res){
2      var uid = req.params.uid
3        , file = req.params.file;
4
5      req.user.mayViewFilesFrom(uid, function(yes){
6        if (yes) {
7          res.sendFile('/uploads/' + uid + '/' + file);
8        } else {
```

```
9            res.status(403).send('Sorry! you cant see that.');
10      }
11    });
12  });
```

- res.sendStatus

Sets the status code of the HTTP answer to the appropriate value. The suitable character sequence is thereby automatically produced. Syntax:

```
res.sendStatus(statusCode)
```

```
1   res.sendStatus(200);
2   // äquivalent zu res.status(200).send('OK')
3   res.sendStatus(403);
4   // äquivalent zu res.status(403).send('Forbidden')
5   res.sendStatus(404);
6   // äquivalent zu res.status(404).send('Not Found')
7   res.sendStatus(500);
8   // äquivalent zu res.status(500).send('Internal Server Error')
```

If a code is produced, which does not admit according to HTTP specification, it is sent nevertheless and the character sequence representation of the code is used:

```
1   res.sendStatus(2000); // equivalent to res.status(2000).send('2000')
```

- res.set

If a head field in the response relies on a certain value. This method can also deal with an object, in order to produce several head fields in one call. Syntax:

```
res.set(field [, value])
```

```
1   res.set('Content-Type', 'text/plain');
2
3   res.set({
4     'Content-Type': 'text/plain',
5     'Content-Length': '123',
6     'ETag': '12345'
7   })
```

For this there is an alians with the name "res.header(field [, value])".

- res.status

Sets the status code of the HTTP response to the appropriate value.
The suitable character sequence is not thereby produced. Syntax:

```
res.status(code)
```

```
1   res.status(403).end();
2   res.status(400).send('Bad Request');
3   res.status(404).sendFile('/absolute/path/to/404.png');
```

- res.type

Sets the head field *Content-Type* to a MIME type. Internally, "mime.lookup()" is used, in order to determine the value. The information of a short spelling is sufficient. If the value contains the slash "/", the value is invariably taken over. Syntax:

```
res.type(type)
```

```
1   res.type('.html');                  // => 'text/html'
2   res.type('html');                   // => 'text/html'
3   res.type('json');                   // => 'application/json'
4   res.type('application/json');       // => 'application/json'
5   res.type('png');                    // => image/png:
```

- res.vary

Adds the 'Vary' head field to a value, if not there yet. Syntax:

```
res.vary(field)
```

```
1   res.vary('User-Agent').render('docs');
```

The API of the Router

This section shows the specific API of the router.

The Router in Detail

A router object is an insulating instance of middleware and routes. It is an application which implements processing functions on the request, recognizes routes, passes on and provides answers. An Express application always has an inserted router:

The router (the part of the application, which processes routes) is a piece of middleware and can be used as app.use() argument. On the highest level, the function Router() in fact serves to produce a new router object.

Produce a new Router

A new router is produced as follows:

```
1   var options = {};
2   var router = express.Router(options);
```

The delivery of the options itself is optional. The following features are available:

Table A-5. *Options of the Router*

Property	Description
caseSensitive	Consider upper and lower case, i.e. */Foo* and */foo* are not the same.
mergeParams	Keeps "req.params" values of the superordinate router. If parameter names overlap, then the name of the parameter of the ch Standard is "false".
strict	Turns on strict Routing. Standard is "false". If this is activated, */foo* and */foo/* won't be the same anymore.

The router permits access to the request like every other middleware component, so that processing can be accomplished promptly with suitable setting of tasks. Those also affect the evaluation of the HTTP verbs (GET, POST, PUT etc.):

```
1   router.use(function(req, res, next) {
2     // Logik des Routers ohne Route
3     next();
4   });
5
6   router.get('/events', function(req, res, next) {
7     // Logik des Routers mit Route '/events'
8   });
```

It is meaningful to use a router for the master URL (root) and to divide the application into a number of smaller miniapplications. In the following example, only the routes with the path "/calender/*" are sent to the router with the name *calRouter*.

```
1   app.use('/calendar', calRouter);
```

Methods

In the following the methods of the router object are described more directly.

- `router.all`

This method functions like all response methods, only that instead of a certain HTTP verb it will react to all verbs. Thus, very simply, a kind of general logic can be developed, which accepts and processes universal requests. General tasks are:

- Authentication
- Authorization
- Caching
- Logging
- Meeting Processing

Note that for this in more extensive applications, also middleware functions can be used. In each case the processing can be continued with next(), so that the action does not have to produce necessarily an output. The following example releases two actions:

```
1   router.all('*', requireAuthentication, loadUser);
```

Alternatively, the agreement can also take place successively:

```
1   router.all('*', requireAuthentication)
2   router.all('*', loadUser);
```

The next example limits the universal access to paths, which begin with *api*:

```
1   router.all('/api/*', requireAuthentication);
```

Further Methods

The methods router.METHOD() react in each way to a concrete HTTP verb. The name for the placeholder *METHOD* is the lower case written version of the verb. GET is thus processed with "get", POST with "post", etc.

Again the path can be limited (first argument) and many callback functions can be indicated.

```
1   router.get('/', function(req, res){
2     res.send('hello world');
3   });
```

In order to implement requests of the kind "GET /commits/71dbb9c" just like "GET /commits/71dbb9c..4c084f9", the following regular expression is suitable as path:

```
1   router.get(/^\/commits\/(\w+)(?:\.\.(\w+))?$/,
2               function(req, res){
3               var from = req.params[0];
4               var to = req.params[1] || 'HEAD';
5               res.send('commit range ' + from + '..' + to);
6               });
```

- router.param

With this method, parameters can be checked. The name of the parameter and a callback function are indicated. The function requires four arguments: Request, Response, Next, and the value of the parameter. The following example shows the access to the parameter *user*. Its value is handed over into *id*.

```
1   router.param('user', function(req, res, next, id) {
2
3     // User ist ein Pseudoobjekt, dass passende Daten enthält
4     User.find(id, function(err, user) {
5       if (err) {
6         next(err);
7       } else if (user) {
8         req.user = user;
9         next();
```

```
10       } else {
11         next(new Error('Nicht gefunden'));
12       }
13     });
14   });
```

The callback function is local to the router, for which it was defined. Callback functions are not passed on in attached apps or routing (Sub apps, Sub router). In addition, they are called only once within a cycle, even if the route fits several times.

```
1    router.param('id', function (req, res, next, id) {
2      console.log('Nur ein Aufruf, auch wenn /:id folgt');
3      next();
4    })
5
6    router.get('/user/:id', function (req, res, next) {
7      console.log('Erste Route');
8      next();
9    });
10
11   router.get('/user/:id', function (req, res) {
12     console.log('Zweite Route');
13     res.end();
14   });
```

- router.route(path)

This method returns an instance of a route. This can be used in order to implement for certain HTTP verbs additional middleware actions. This can be reached also by renewed information of the route; however, you must then also write the route several times and thus may experience possibilities of error as a result of typing errors.

```
1    var router = express.Router();
2
3    router.param('user_id', function(req, res, next, id) {
4      // Muster, hier folgt ein Datenbankaufruf o.ä.
5      req.user = {
6        id: id,
7        name: 'TJ'
8      };
9      next();
10   });
11
12   router.route('/users/:user_id')
13       .all(function(req, res, next) {
14         // Alle Verben
15         next();
16       })
17       .get(function(req, res, next) {
18         res.json(req.user);
19       })
20       .put(function(req, res, next) {
```

```
21        // Beispiel
22          req.user.name = req.params.name;
23        // Speichern folgt hier (nicht gezeigt)
24          res.json(req.user);
25        })
26        .post(function(req, res, next) {
27          next(new Error('nicht implementiert'));
28        })
29        .delete(function(req, res, next) {
30          next(new Error('nicht implementiert'));
31        });
```

The path /*users*:user_id of the route is here used several times for different HTTP verbs.

- `router.use`

This method agrees upon a middleware function. Optionally a path can be indicated. Without information on the path the master path "/" is used. That is comparable with app.use(); the use is identical.

```
1   var express = require('express');
2   var app = express();
3   var router = express.Router();
4
5   // Einfacher Logger: Alle Anfragen gehen zuerst durch diese Methode
6   router.use(function(req, res, next) {
7     console.log('%s %s %s', req.method, req.url, req.path);
8     next();
9   });
10
11  // Nur für Pfade, die mit /bar beginnen
12  router.use('/bar', function(req, res, next) {
13    // ... Middleware-Funktion vor der Verarbeitung
14    next();
15  });
16
17  // Wird immer aufgerufen
18  router.use(function(req, res, next) {
19    res.send('Hello World');
20  });
21
22  app.use('/foo', router);
23
24  app.listen(3000);
```

The actual path is not of importance and not visible for the middleware function. The idea behind it essentially is that functions can be implemented independently of the path.

The execution of the functions is determined by the order of the definition. A function is implemented sequentially.

```
1   var logger = require('morgan');
2
3   router.use(logger());
```

```
4    router.use(express.static(__dirname + '/public'));
5    router.use(function(req, res){
6      res.send('Hello');
7    });
```

Consider the following if you want to prevent the logging for static files. But further steps of the middleware for those files shall still be implemented. In addition, you shift the definition for static files ("express.static") simply before the agreement of the middleware function:

```
1    router.use(express.static(__dirname + '/public'));
2    router.use(logger());
3    router.use(function(req, res){
4      res.send('Hello');
5    });
```

Likewise, it can be determined by the order in which folders the search will start first. In the following example the folder *public* is scanned first. If the router finds something, the request is worked on. If the router does not find anything, it searches in the next folder. Also, here the sequence in the script file is determining.

```
1    app.use(express.static(__dirname + '/public'));
2    app.use(express.static(__dirname + '/files'));
3    app.use(express.static(__dirname + '/uploads'));
```

The method router.use() supports in addition the designated parameter (*name:* etc.), so that following steps can access this data.

Further libraries

With some further libraries the functionality of the Express router can be extended in a smart way.

- Namespace Based Routing

- Resource Based Routing

Namespace Based Routing

In order to understand the sense of Namespaces, first a typical example of a set of routes is to be demonstrated:

```
1    app.get('/articles/', function(req, res) { ... });
2    app.get('/articles/new', function(req, res) { ... });
3    app.get('/articles/edit/:id', function(req, res) { ... });
4    app.get('/articles/delete/:id', function(req, res) { ... });
5    app.get('/articles/2013', function(req, res) { ... });
6    app.get('/articles/2013/jan/', function(req, res) { ... });
7    app.get('/articles/2013/jan/nodejs', function(req, res) { ... });
```

With increasing number of routes and in each case, the belonging path elements, it becomes clear that the expenditure is immense. However, above all it is remarkable that many path components are identical. Parts of the paths are repeated endlessly, as in the example the name *articles*.

Now it would be smart to define a good basis path to the list that not only lists the relative components, but in addition, serves name spaces. Thus, only a simplification or a shortening of the spelling concerns the routes. Less writing, of course, also means less errors.

Express has an included function for this, however a plug-in is available which does it way better. You can install it via the Node package manager **npm** as follows:

```
$  npm  install express-namespace
```

Now the file *app.js* must be adapted, so that the routes can use the Namespace:

Listing A-7. app.js

```
1   var http = require('http');
2   var express = require('express');
3
4   // express-namespace muss geladen werden, bevor die App instanziiert\
5    wird
6   var namespace = require('express-namespace');
7   var app = express();
8
9   app.use(app.router);
10
11  // Definition of Namespace
12  app.namespace('/articles', function() {
13
14    app.get('/', function(req, res) {
15      res.send('index of articles');
16    });
17
18    app.post('/new', function(req, res) {
19      res.send('new article');
20    });
21
22    app.put('/edit/:id', function(req, res) {
23      res.send('edit article ' + req.params.id);
24    });
25
26    app.delete('/delete/:id', function(req, res) {
27      res.send('delete article ' + req.params.id);
28    });
29
30    app.get('/2013', function(req, res) {
31      res.send('articles from 2013');
32    });
33
34    // Nested Namespace
35    app.namespace('/2013/jan', function() {
36
37      app.get('/', function(req, res) {
38        res.send('articles from jan 2013');
39      });
40
```

```
41      app.get('/nodejs', function(req, res) {
42        res.send('articles about Node from jan 2013');
43      });
44    });
45
46  });
47
48  http.createServer(app).listen(3000, function() {
49    console.log('App started');
50  });
```

After the loading of the application the following routes are available:

- http://localhost:3000/articles/

- http://localhost:3000/articles/edit/4

- http://localhost:3000/articles/delete/4

- http://localhost:3000/articles/2013

- http://localhost:3000/articles/2013/jan

- http://localhost:3000/articles/2013/jan/nodejs

Name spaces support–like all routes–both placeholders in character strings and regular expressions in the literal spelling

Resource-Based Routing

There is a further approach for the Routing, which works more object-oriented. The idea is based on the consideration to get objects ready which contain the actions. The routes lead to these actions.

They provide thus more paths, but define objects. These objects are regarded as sources.

It is smart to provide these objects as models of the domain. By domain here is referred to the technical domain–thus, its purpose to the user. Resources are in this sense things such as users, pictures, articles, books, or also forum contributions. Usually it acts in the illustration of the data source. With resource-based routing HTTPs verbs with path samples are combined.

The following table shows which verbs are suitable for which actions.

Table A-6. *Resource Based Routing*

HTTP Verb	Path	Module Methods	Description
GET	/users	index	List users
GET	/users/new	new	Form for the creation of a new users
POST	/users	create	Process form data
GET	/users/:id	show	Show users with the ID :id
GET	/users/:id/edit	edit	Show process form for users:id
PUT	/users/:id	update	Process the changes on the user
DELETE	/users/:id	destroy	Delete the user with the ID :id

This implicit link between verbs and routes and the actions is not standard in the Express environment. The plug-in *express-resource* is necessary. Install this with the help of the Node package manager **npm** as follows:

```
$ npm install express-resource
```

Now a module is provided which can treat the routes. If you follow the *user* example, the accommodation in a file is suitable for *users.js* (for the sake of the order, the name is not relevant). The implementation then looks as follows:

```
1   exports.index = function(req, res) {
2     res.send('index of users');
3   };
4
5   exports.new = function(req, res) {
6     res.send('form for new user');
7   };
8
9   exports.create = function(req, res) {
10    res.send('handle form for new user');
11  };
12
13  exports.show = function(req, res) {
14    res.send('show user ' + req.params.user);
15  };
16
17  exports.edit = function(req, res) {
18    res.send('form to edit user ' + req.params.user);
19  };
20
21  exports.update = function(req, res) {
22    res.send('handle form to edit user ' + req.params.user);
23  };
24
25  exports.destroy = function(req, res) {
26    res.send('delete user ' + req.params.user);
27  };
```

In the well known *app.js* the use of the module will have to be agreed upon:

```
1   var http = require('http');
2   var express = require('express');
3   // express-resource must be loaded before the app-instance
4   var resource = require('express-resource');
5
6   var app = express();
7
8   app.use(app.router);
9
10  // Laden der Aktions-Datei
11  app.resource('users', require('./users.js'));
12
```

```
13   http.createServer(app).listen(3000, function() {
14     console.log('App gestartet');
15   });
```

After the start the actions are available under the following routes

- http://localhost:3000/users

- http://localhost:3000/users/new

- http://localhost:3000/users/5

- http://localhost:3000/users/5/edit

In order to use the POST, PUT or DELETE action, you either use a tool like Fiddler or Curl, with which requests can be assembled manually. Or you program the equal suitable inquiries in the browser by means of AJAX libraries, like jFLery or AngularJS.

In relation to the previously shown version, you save explicit indicating of the routes and thus some time at work and sources of errors.

The Pug API

Pug is a package that contains a function as Programming Interface (API) apart from processing templates. This API subsequently will be briefly described.

API Options

Each method of the API accepts options, which are handed over as JSON structure:

```
1    {
2      filename: string,
3      doctype: string,
4      pretty: boolean | string,
5      self: boolean,
6      debug: boolean,
7      compileDebug: boolean,
8      cache: boolean,
9      compiler: class,
10     parser: class,
11     globals: Array.<string>
12   }
```

The individual parameters have the following meaning:

- **filename**

  The file name; is shown for example in exceptions

- **doctype**

  The Doctype, if this will not be indicated as part of a template

- **pretty**

Shows whether blanks are to be added to the spent HTML or not, in order to produce readable code. If a character string is indicated, this is the value, which is used for engaging, e.g. '\t'. self "self" name area for local variable (according to standard false).

- **debug**

  Log expenditures after "stdout"

- **compileDebug**

  The source code is transferred into the rendered output cache Functions are called. The key is the file name of the template.

- **compiler**

  An alternative compiler can be indicated.

- **parser**

  An alternative Parser can be indicated.

- **globals**

  Global variables, which are announced in all templates

API Functions

In all functions the parameter "options" is the option object described before. Not all options are meaningful in all cases. pug.compile(source, options) — this function translates Pug code, so that this can be implemented several times with different values. A function returns, which can be implemented. The instruction on line 2 provides the function, on line 3 this is then implemented.

```
1  var pug = require('pug');
2  var fn = pug.compile('p pug is cool!', options);
3  var html = fn(locals);
```

This script produces the following output:

```
<p>pug is cool!</p>
```

pug.compileFile(path, options)

This function translates Pug code from a file, so that this can be implemented several times with different values. A function returns, which can be implemented. "sourcepath" is the path to the Pug file. The instruction on line 2 provides the function, on line 3 this is then implemented.

```
1  var pug = require('pug');
2  var fn = pug.compileFile('views/index.pug', options);
3  var html = fn(locals);
```

This script produces the following output: If the file is *index.pug*, the text "p pug is cool!" contains:

```
<p>pug ist cool!</p>
```

pug.compileClient(source, options)

Here a JavaScript function will be implemented and rendered, then later the client page can be provided and the HTML produced.

```
1   var pug = require('pug');
2
3   // Create Function
4   var fn = pug.compileClient('p pug is cool!', options);
5
6   // Render Function
7   var html = fn(locals);
```

The return is then pure JavaScript:

```
1   function template(locals) {
2     return "<p>pug is cool!</p>";
3   }
```

pug.compileClientWithDependenciesTracked(source, options)

This method corresponds to the preceding method compileClient, however it produces an object, which has the following structure:

```
1   {
2     'body': 'function (locals) {...}',
3     'dependencies': ['filename.pug']
4   }
```

Thus, changes at source files can be supervised. Otherwise the simple variant is to be preferred.

pug.compileFileClient(path, options)

Here a JavaScript function will be implemented and rendered, then later the client page can be provided and the HTML produced.

The source must be present as file. The option object has a further parameter name. This determines the name of the function, which is produced and can be called by the client. Here an example with the source file *pugFile.pug*:

```
1   h1 This is a template
2   h2 By #{author}
```

This is now translated dynamically (line 4):

```
1   var fs = require('fs');
2   var pug = require('pug');
3
4   var jsOut = pug.compileFileClient('/views/pugFile.pug',
5                   {
6                       name: "templateFunction"
7                   });
```

fs   The example uses the standard module "fs" from the node.js distribution. You'll find more information in the chapters about Node.js.

Imagine you want all of your templates in one file and to translate these, while subsequently giving them to the client. Then the output of the last example jsOut can be stored as follows:

```
1   fs.writeFileSync("templates.js", jsOut);
```

The file *templates.js*, which develops from it contains the function defined below as *templateFunction*:

```
1    function templateFunction(locals) {
2     var buf = [];
3     var pug_mixins = {};
4     var pug_interp;
5
6     var locals_for_with = (locals || {});
7
8     (function (author) {
9     buf.push("<h1>This is a template </h1><h2>From "
10            + (pug.escape((pug_interp = author) == null ? '' : pug_inte\
11            rp))
12            + "</h2>");
13    }.call(this, "author" in locals_for_with ?
14    locals_for_with.author : typeof author !== "undefined" ?
15    author : undefined)
16    );
17
18    return buf.join("");
19    }
```

For this to function, the runtime environment of Pug must be available. It is available under the name runtime.js. In the HTML of the clients, this then looks as follows:

```
1    <!DOCTYPE html>
2    <html>
3    <head>
4     <script src="/runtime.js"></script>
5     <script src="/templates.js"></script>
6    </head>
7
8    <body>
9      <h1>This is a template</h1>
10
11     <script type="text/javascript">
12       var html = window.templateFunction({author: "Joerg"});
13       var div = document.createElement("div");
14       div.innerHTML = html;
15       document.body.appendChild(div);
16     </script>
17    </body>
18    </html>
```

pug.render(source, options)

This function renders directly in HTML:

```
1   var pug = require('pug');
2   var html = pug.render('p Pug ist cool!', options);
```

Now the HTML looks like this:

```
<p>Pug ist cool!</p>
```

pug.renderFile(filename, options)

This function renders directly in HTML, too. It uses a file as input:

```
1   var pug = require('pug');
2   var html = pug.renderFile('views/file.pug', options);
```

Index

© Jörg Krause 2017
J. Krause, *Programming Web Applications with Node, Express and Pug*, DOI 10.1007/978-1-4842-2511-0

Get the eBook for only $4.99!

Why limit yourself?

Now you can take the weightless companion with you wherever you go and access your content on your PC, phone, tablet, or reader.

Since you've purchased this print book, we are happy to offer you the eBook for just $4.99.

Convenient and fully searchable, the PDF version enables you to easily find and copy code—or perform examples by quickly toggling between instructions and applications.

To learn more, go to http://www.apress.com/us/shop/companion or contact support@apress.com.

Printed in the United States
By Bookmasters